OECD Studies on Water

The Governance of Water Regulators

Please cite this publication as:
OECD (2015), *The Governance of Water Regulators*, OECD Studies on Water, OECD Publishing, Paris.
http://dx.doi.org/10.1787/9789264231092-en

ISBN 978-92-64-23108-5 (print)
ISBN 978-92-64-23109-2 (PDF)

Series: OECD Studies on Water
ISSN 2224-5073 (print)
ISSN 2224-5081 (online)

Photo credits: Cover © Brooman – Fotolia.com.

Corrigenda to OECD publications may be found on line at: *www.oecd.org/about/publishing/corrigenda.htm*.

Foreword

This report is part of a project of the Regulatory Policy Committee (RPC) on *Applying Better Regulation for the Water Sector*, which contributes to the OECD project on Water Policies for Future Cities. It has been developed in close co-operation with the water regulators of the OECD Network of Economic Regulators (NER). The NER provides the opportunity for regulators to gain access to their peers, including from other sectors, and to discuss how to harness the range of regulatory governance principles and practices developed by the OECD for the benefit of interested water authorities. In addition, the OECD offers the possibility of tapping into the wide range of expertise and policy communities involved in all aspects of the water sector of the Horizontal Water Programme (www.oecd.org/water) and the Water Governance Initiative (www.oecd.org/env/watergovernanceprogramme.htm#WaterGovInitiative).

This report describes the features of a sample of regulatory bodies set up to regulate the provision of urban drinking water and wastewater services (WWS), including their various functions and powers, and their institutional setting and internal organisation. It is based on a survey of water regulators carried out between September 2013 and September 2014 to investigate the following areas: *i)* institutional setting; *ii)* mandates, roles and core regulatory functions; *iii)* internal organisation; *iv)* accountability mechanisms; and *v)* use of tools and mechanisms to ensure regulatory quality. The report uses the *OECD Best Practice Principles for Regulatory Policy: The Governance of Regulators*, as well as the body of knowledge and country practices developed by the OECD on water, as the basis for the analysis.

The results of this work provide the first sectoral application of the OECD *Best Practice Principles for Regulatory Policy: The Governance of Regulators*), and complements the results of the OECD Product Market Regulation (PMR) Survey on network regulators. The work also contributes to OECD efforts to update the existing legal instruments and standards on water. This report describes the features of water regulators to foster the sharing of practices and inform the establishment of new regulators in countries that choose this path. It should not be construed as a recommendation to establish independent regulators in all country contexts.

The report was extensively discussed by the NER and presented at the Forum of Water Regulators co-organised by the International Water Association (IWA) and the Portuguese water regulator (ERSAR) in 2014. It was circulated to the RPC and the Water Governance Initiative and other stakeholders for comments. The report was launched at the 7th World Water Forum held in April 2015 in Korea.

Acknowledgements

This publication was drafted and co-ordinated by Céline Kauffmann, Deputy Head, under the guidance and supervision of Nick Malyshev, Head of the OECD Regulatory Policy Division, and under the responsibility of Rolf Alter, Director of the Directorate for Public Governance and Territorial Development. It benefitted from substantial inputs from Carine Viac. Dambudzo Muzenda was instrumental in developing the survey to water regulators and Laura Seiffert provided excellent statistical assistance. The report benefitted from strong support and guidance from the water regulators of the NER, in particular ERSAR (Portugal), AEEGSI (Italy), the regulation unit of the Flemish Environment Agency (Belgium/Flanders), PUC (Latvia), and the Water Regulatory Authority of Albania. Inputs and constructive comments were provided by all contributing regulators (a list is provided in Annex A), the Ministry of Infrastructure and the Environment of the Netherlands and Aquafed, as well as by colleagues from the OECD Secretariat (Aziza Akhmouch, Filippo Cavassini, Xavier Leflaive and Faisal Naru). The report was prepared for publication by Jennifer Stein.

The Regulatory Policy Committee and its subsidiary body, the Network of Economic Regulators, are supported by staff within the Regulatory Policy Division of the Public Governance and Territorial Development Directorate. The OECD Public Governance and Territorial Development Directorate's unique emphasis on institutional design and policy implementation supports mutual learning and diffusion of best practice in different societal and market conditions. The goal is to help countries build better government systems and implement policies at both national and regional level that lead to sustainable economic and social development. The directorate's mission is to help governments at all levels design and implement strategic, evidence-based and innovative policies to strengthen public governance, respond effectively to diverse and disruptive economic, social and environmental challenges and deliver on governments' commitments to citizens.

Table of contents

Tables

Figures

Acronyms and abbreviations

AEEGSI	Autorità per l'energia elettrica il gas e il Sistema idrico (Italian Regulatory Authority for Electricity Gas and Water)
AGERGS	Agência Estadual de Regulação dos Serviços Públicos, Delegados do Rio Grande do Sul (State Agency for the Regulation of Public Services of Rio Grande do Sul, Brazil)
ANRSC	Autoritatea Națională de Reglementare pentru Serviciile Comunitare de Utilități Publice (National Regulatory Authority for Municipal Services of Romania)
CER	Commission for Energy Regulation of Ireland
CRA (Colombia)	Comisión de Regulación de Agua Potable y Saneamiento Básico (Regulatory Commission for Water and Sanitation, Colombia)
CRA (Mozambique)	Conselho de Regulaçao de Aguas (Water and Sanitation Regulatory Council, Mozambique)
DEFRA	Department for Environment, Food and Rural Affairs, United Kingdom
EPA	Environmental Protection Agency
ERAWA	Economic Regulation Authority of Western Australia
ERSAR	Entidade Reguladora dos Servicios de Aguas e Residuos (The Water and Waste Services Regulation Authority of Portugal)
ICRC	Independent Competition and Regulatory Commission of the Australian Capital Territory
IPART	Independent Pricing and Regulatory Tribunal of New South Wales
NIAUR	Northern Ireland Authority for Utility Regulator
NSW	New South Wales
OFWAT	Water Services Regulation Authority for England and Wales
ONEMA	Office National de l'Eau et des Milieux Aquatiques (French National Agency for Water and Aquatic Environment)
PMU	Project Management Unit of Jordan
PSRC	Public Services Regulatory Commission of the Republic of Armenia
PUC	Public Utilities Commission of Latvia
RIA	Regulatory Impact Analysis
SCWRM	National Commission of the State Public Utilities Regulation of Ukraine
SEWRC	State Energy and Water Regulatory Commission of Bulgaria
SISS	Superintendencia de Servicio Sanitarios (Water Regulator of Chile)
SUNASS	Superintendencia Nacional de Servicios de Saneamiento (Water Regulator of Peru)
URSEA	Unidad Reguladora Servicios Energia y Agua (Water Regulator of Uruguay)
VMM	Vlaamse MilieiMaatschappij (Flemish Environment Agency)
WISC	Water Industry Commission for Scotland
WWRO	Water and Wastewater Regulatory Office of Kosovo
WWS	Water and wastewater services

Executive summary

This report describes the governance arrangements, operational modalities and use of regulatory tools across a sample of 34 bodies responsible for regulating the provision of drinking water and wastewater services [hereafter referred to as water regulators], based on the OECD *Best Practice Principles for Regulatory Policy: The Governance of Regulators*.

As the responses to the OECD survey illustrate the establishment of water regulators is both recent and a consistent trend among OECD and non-OECD countries. Apart from a few exceptions (based in the US), most responding regulators were established in the past 25 years. A water regulator is generally established to protect the public interest as part of broader reforms to make service providers more accountable, to establish an independent price-setting process and to bring regulatory expertise into the public sector. In the territories under study, the establishment of a dedicated regulatory body for water services is seen as responding to the need of a complex sector – prone to market failures and where regulatory responsibilities are fragmented – by promoting transparency, policy coherence and co-ordination, continuity, predictability and credibility of decision-making (in particular concerning tariff setting) and accountability to users.

Survey responses also show the importance of multi-sector regulators, which constitute two thirds of survey respondents. Among the six new regulators in the water field since 2010, five cover more than one sector. For the majority of multi-sector regulators, responsibility for water is bundled with that for energy. Water has generally been added to the portfolio of an already established regulator in order to benefit from the credibility of the existing structure. The opportunity for making cost savings by sharing administrative and support services with other sectors, and for creating synergies, has also been an important driver for establishing the multi-sector regulators in the sample.

The 34 water regulators surveyed have generally adopted many of the good governance principles and practices identified in the *OECD Best Practice Principles for Regulatory Policy: The Governance of Regulators*. In particular, when it comes to their institutional settings and governance arrangements, water regulators generally display legitimacy, clarity of roles and responsibilities, and accountability grounded in legislative instruments. The descriptive analysis shows that co-ordination with entities with related responsibilities, however, is mainly pursued on an ad hoc basis rather than through systematic and institutionalised mechanisms. Improvement in this area would increase the clarity and the legitimacy of the regulatory framework.

Most water regulators display functions and powers that are in line with their objectives. Based on the survey answers, they have a critical role in four main areas: *i)* economic regulation; *ii)* data collection and performance monitoring related to water services; *iii)* enforcement of regulations and standards; and *iv)* customer engagement and protection. Based on these functions and powers, water regulators should play a key role in ensuring transparency in the water sector and in making the sector more user-centric and accountable to the public. They are a source of information on the performance of water utilities and water systems, as well as on the rules, regulations and other strategic choices in service delivery. They also constitute a critical link in the regulatory governance cycle in support of the concrete implementation of government policies, by ensuring compliance and credibility of the regulatory framework.

Operational practices of water regulators vary widely. However, more needs to be done to link the roles and responsibilities of water regulators and their operational modalities. Similarly, regulators use a wide variety of different practices and tools in carrying out their activities and discharging their functions. More in-depth work and exchange of information, including with regulators outside of the water sector, on key performance indicators and benchmarking frameworks for instance, or on processes and methodologies of tariff regulation, would help refine the understanding of the critical challenges and the identification of the good practices.

In their use of regulatory tools, water regulators show a strong culture of consultation. While there is a need to keep the allocation of responsibilities across authorities clear and not to infringe on the independence of independent regulatory bodies, regulators' culture of proximity with the regulated and the users could be better harnessed by governments to improve regulations in the sector. Other areas, in particular evaluation of regulatory impacts, could be further strengthened. Regulators are in a privileged position to monitor the impacts of regulations and regulatory decisions and are able to use the information to continuously update and improve regulatory tools used in the sector. However, a number of regulators (although a minority) reported that they do not carry out *ex ante* impact assessment of their regulatory decisions and a majority are not involved in *ex post* evaluation of regulatory impacts.

This report provides a snapshot of regulators' governance and practices as of September 2014. However, the water service sector is a fast-evolving area of policy making. The activities, powers and organisation of regulators change as the water industry reforms and regulatory bodies mature. The OECD will continue to track new developments in the governance of regulators.

Chapter 1

Overview of regulatory frameworks for water services in selected countries

Countries regulate the provision of water services in different ways. There is a large literature that reviews the different regulatory models in use globally. While a detailed description of these models is outside the scope of this report, this chapter focuses on describing the main regulatory models for water services. It identifies the establishment of dedicated regulatory bodies as a growing trend among countries and sheds some light on the motivations behind this trend.

Countries regulate the dimensions of water services (the network, quality, service delivery, pricing etc.) in different ways. One recent trend, the development of dedicated regulatory bodies for drinking water and wastewater services (WWS), stands out as a consistent response to some of the challenges to regulating water services (including the fragmentation of roles and responsibilities in the sector and the difficult political economy of tariff setting). On the whole, however, dedicated water regulators remain at earlier stages of development compared to other utility sectors and a number of countries and territories are still considering whether and how to establish them. This report aims to inform this new development by drawing lessons from the existing experience of established regulatory bodies in the water sector.

The challenges faced in the drinking water and wastewater service sector

The WWS sector is a typical example of a **monopolist sector**. Water companies constitute natural monopolies since the costs of production are lesser in the case of a single producer for a given spectrum of demand (Marques, 2010). Consequently, the WWS market is characterised by a low level of competition and important restrictions on the entrance of new players. Regulation is justified on the ground that it ought to prevent market power issues arising from a natural monopoly and to protect customers. In the absence of regulation, water operators can be tempted to neglect the quality of services and to apply water tariffs which are unreasonably high compared to the production costs.

The WWS sector also displays important **asymmetry of information**. The water operators own information which the responsible public authorities and the consumers do not have access to. This asymmetry of information may lead to market abuse by the monopolist operators and cause mistrust amongst consumers with regard to the quality of services provided (Marques, 2010). An easy and transparent access to WWS data can reduce the risks of asymmetric information.

The water sector needs to **balance a range of economic, social and environmental interests**. Water is essential for the lives, health and social protection of citizens. As a consequence, water services must fulfil a number of requirements such as the principle of universality, continuity, quality of service, equality of access, affordability and transparency. At the same time, the provision of WWS services has a cost – important investments and management and operating costs are involved – that needs to be covered in the most efficient way to ensure its sustainability over time. The management and trade-off across various interests justifies public intervention.

The water sector generates **important externalities**, in particular in relation to public health, the economy and the environment. The quality of water has strong impacts on public health, which justify the involvement of the ministry of health to define and set the quality standards for drinking water and wastewater treatment. The way wastewater is treated can also impact the environment, and, if ignored or badly managed, generate pollution and negatively impact other productive activities (farming, fishing and tourism). Therefore, in most countries, the ministry of environment is usually responsible for setting the quality standards for wastewater treatment.

WWS are often characterised by a **fragmentation of actors**. This fragmentation is both horizontal and vertical. At the horizontal level, several line ministries and other governmental agencies are involved in the regulation of water services, including typically ministries of environment (for managing water pollution); ministries of health (for setting and monitoring water quality standards) and, in some cases, the ministries of economics and finance (for investment and tariff regulation). At the vertical level, WWS are characterised by multi-level regulatory governance from supra- to sub-national levels. The EU provides an illustration of supra-national regulatory powers in the water service sector, notably through the EU Water Directive. At sub-national level, municipalities are generally responsible for providing and managing water and wastewater service delivery. In practice, OECD (2011) shows that the multiplicity of actors across ministries and public agencies, between levels of government and at the sub-national level intrinsically raises multi-level governance challenges. With so many participants, a clear definition of roles and responsibilities, as well as the establishment of co-ordination mechanisms, are therefore crucial to manage effectively and efficiently water services.

An overview of regulatory functions for WWS

Market failures and critical features of the water sector justify the establishment of high quality regulatory framework to serve the public interest at least cost for all actors involved. There is a large spectrum of regulatory functions routinely performed in relation to water services. Regulation of water services is not only about tariff regulation, it involves other functions, such as the monitoring of standards for access to and quality of services, the establishment of efficiency incentives, collection of information and monitoring of performance, and the organisation of users' participation. In order to take stock of these various functions and support policy making in this area, the OECD has developed a typology of regulatory functions (Table 1.1). This preliminary typology was tested and used to analyse the WWS regulatory framework in a number of countries (including Mexico, Jordan and Tunisia) (OECD, 2013, 2014b, 2014c) and constituted the basis for the questions on the functions of water regulators in the survey.

Table 1.1. **Typology of regulatory functions for WWS**

Type of regulatory functions	Definition
Tariff regulation	Establishing a tariff methodology and/or setting and updating prices or supervising the tariff setting process, determining tariffs by consumer group, establishing caps on revenues or rate of return on investment.
Quality standards for drinking water	Setting quality standards for drinking water and/or monitoring compliance.
Quality standards for wastewater treatment	Setting quality standards for wastewater treatment and wastewater discharges and/or monitoring compliance.
Defining public service obligations/social regulation	Setting public service obligations (including requirements on access to services) and performance requirements for operators.
Defining technical/industry and service standards	Developing the standards that underpin the technical modalities and level of service delivery.
Setting incentives for efficient use of water resources	Establishing incentives or specific schemes to promote efficient water resource use.
Setting incentives for efficient investment	Establishing incentives or specific schemes to promote efficient investment.
Promoting innovative technologies	Establishing incentives or specific schemes to promote innovative technologies.

Table 1.1. **Typology of regulatory functions for WWS** (*cont.*)

Type of regulatory functions	Definition
Promoting demand management	Establishing incentives or specific schemes to promote reduced water demands.
Analysing water utilities' investment plans/business plans	In some cases, the regulator may be asked to approve the business plan or the investment plan of utilities.
Information and data gathering	Collecting data from operators, undertaking market research to identify trends and potential risks.
Monitoring of service delivery performance	Monitoring of the performance of water services against a set of targets or of performance indicators. This can involve benchmarking water utilities.
Licensing of water operators	Granting or approving licences for the operation of water systems.
Supervision of contracts with utilities/private actors	The obligations granted by the public authorities to a specific utility may be detailed in a specific contract (it is usually the case when a private actor is brought in). The regulator may be tasked with the supervision of the contract.
Supervising utilities' financing activities	Monitoring the financial schemes of water utilities (e.g. bond issuance, equity investments).
Carrying management audits on utilities	Auditing and /or approving the business plans of utilities.
Customer engagement	Consulting with customers on regulatory issues; communicating regulatory decisions to the public.
Consumer protection and dispute resolution	Handling consumer complaints about regulated entities.
Advice and advocacy	Providing advice for policy making and project implementation; identifying opportunities for reforms, encouraging improvements to the regulatory framework.

Regulatory functions for WWS as identified in the OECD typology (Table 1.1) can be of a different nature, some purely economic, some environmental and others embracing social issues, such as equity, affordability, universal coverage. The regulatory functions do not necessarily have to be in the hands of a single institution responsible for all of them. However, they need to be clearly spelt out and allocated to avoid overlap and incoherence. They also need to be clearly differentiated from the roles of other authorities and bodies, such as the policy roles of government or the role in service provision of utilities (public or private).

The variety of regulatory arrangements across countries

Countries have adopted different types of regulatory frameworks to ensure that the various regulatory functions in relation to water services are performed – the establishment of a dedicated regulatory body is one of several possible organisations for the sector. There is a large literature that reviews the different regulatory models in use globally. A detailed description of all the models is outside the scope of this report. However, to situate the focus of this report, the main regulatory models for WWS are described following OECD (2009). Leaving aside self-regulation, there are mainly four regulatory models: 1) regulation by government; 2) regulation by contract, which specifies the regulatory regimes in legal instruments (usually referred to as the French model); 3) independent regulation where independence has three dimensions: independence of decision making, of management and of financing (usually referred to as the Anglo-American model), and 4) outsourcing regulatory functions to third parties, which makes use of external contractors to perform activities such as tariff reviews, benchmarking, dispute resolution.

In the first model, the public sector is responsible for the management of the water services and owns the assets. The provision of the WWS is usually delegated to public water operators while the regulatory functions are carried out directly by the State at its different levels (central, regional, municipal). This organisational model prevails in the Netherlands (Box 1.1) and, to a lesser extent, in Germany (Box 1.2).

Box 1.1. The regulatory framework for WWS in the Netherlands

In the Netherlands, drinking water services are provided by 10 drinking water companies (all public limited companies), sewage collection is entrusted to the 393 municipalities (as of 1 January 2025) and wastewater treatment is carried out by the 23 regional water authorities. Regulation of water services is performed by various public institutions through cooperative governance (OECD, 2014). The Minister of Infrastructure and the Environment bears the ultimate responsibility, including to the parliament, for water management overall. Other institutions are accountable for their respective tasks to their own democratic elected fora: the provincial and municipal councils and the assemblies of the regional water authorities (23). The planning system provides the tool to harmonise the visions and strategies of these institutions. The hierarchy that exists between the layers of government is regulated by law. National government supervises provinces, which have in turn supervisory powers over local governments (water authorities and municipalities).

Drinking water companies are supervised by their public shareholders (municipalities and provinces). According to the Drinking water Act, the Minister of Infrastructure and the Environment sets conditions for continuity, quality, and expediency. The Authority Consumers and Markets (ACM) advises the Minister on tariffs and the costs of capital allowance of drinking water companies. In doing so, the ACM involves the Human Environment and Transport Inspectorate, which supervises drinking water quality.

OECD (2014a) identifies the collection of information and benchmarking as critical elements of water policy in the Netherlands. There are 3 processes that aim to monitor performance, enforcement and compliance and apply to municipalities, drinking water companies and regional water authorities:

- A benchmarking of regional water authorities is carried out by the Dutch Association of Regional Water Authorities every 2 years.
- The performance of drinking water companies is benchmarked every 3 years under the responsibility of the Ministry of Infrastructure and the Environment.
- The performance of municipalities in managing urban drainage and sewerage is benchmarked every 3 years.

An additional joint monitoring system (Water in Beeld), managed by the Ministry of Infrastructure and the Environment, provides parliament an overview of the extent to which policy targets are met, on a yearly basis. The responsible institutions themselves are accountable for the quality of data provided. Encouraging incentives to meet joint policy targets, if need be, can be tailored to the issues to be solved. As an example, the minister established a visitation commission in 2014 to report on the progress made on cooperation between municipalities and water authorities, where substantial cost reductions need to be realised in the transport and treatment of wastewater.

Sources: Ministry of Infrastructure and the Environment of the Netherlands; OECD (2014a), *Water Governance in the Netherlands: Fit for the Future?*, OECD Studies on Water, OECD Publishing, Paris, http://dx.doi.org/10.1787/9789264102637-en.

Box 1.2. The regulatory framework for WWS in Germany

In Germany, responsibility for regulating water supply and wastewater is shared between the EU, the federal government, state governments (*Länder*) and the municipalities. The federal government is in charge of establishing the water framework laws, in particular the Ministry for Economy and Labour, the Ministry for Healthcare and Social Security and the Ministry for Environment. The federal states (16 *Länder*) regulate the WWS in their respective territories; and municipalities ensure sewage services, and depending on the water sector law in their Land, the supply of drinking water (Massarutto *et al.*, 2012).

Compared to other countries, the water sector is fragmented (across 13 364 municipalities) and comprises over 6 560 water supply utilities and 6 700 waste water companies (Massarutto, 2012). WWS operators can be either public- or private-law entities. The share of public-private-partnerships models in total water supply has increased over the last years (Wackerbauer, 2009). However, the municipalities have remained most of the time the majority shareholder to keep their influence on strategic decision (Guerin-Schneider *et al.*, 2002).

The German system functions essentially without a formal and independent regulatory authority but some forms of price controls exist. When the entity in charge of the provision of WWS is under public law, price setting takes place according to the cost-covering principles and is approved by the municipality. In case of controversy, an appeal can be made to an administrative tribunal. When the entity works under private law, the regional antitrust authority can make an enquiry if it suspects unfair pricing practices.

Since 2005, forms of voluntary benchmarking have developed, mostly at the level of the *Länder*. Some 1 800 German water and energy companies are benchmarked against a range of performance indicators (e.g. quality of drinking water, quality of service, security of supply, sustainability of water production and consumption, costs, investments, profits, tariffs). This self-regulation through voluntary benchmarking is conducted by the German Association of Energy and Water Industries.

Sources: Guerin-Schneider *et al.* (2002), Massarutto *et al.* (2012), "Financial Economies of Scale in the Water Sector", Research Report, IEFE, Boconni University, www.iefe.unibocconi.it; Wackerbauer, J. (2009), "The Water Sector in Germany", *Working Paper*, CIRIEC No. 2009/11, November; German Association of Energy and Water Industries (Bundesverband der Energie und Wasserwirtschaft e. V., Berlin), www.bdew.de/internet.nsf/id/de_benchmarking_learning_from_the_best_comparison_of_performance_indicators_in_the_german_water_ind/$file/100301_bdew_benchmarking_broschuere_wa_in_englisch.pdf (accessed 31 March 2014).

In a number of other countries, public authorities are responsible for WWS regulation but the provision of water services can be delegated to private operators through contract agreements. The contract agreements establish the set of rights and obligations for each contracting authorities. The provision of WWS is awarded to private companies following public tenders. WWS infrastructure remains within the public domain. The "French model" of regulation by contract (Box 1.3) originated in France in the nineteenth century and expanded rapidly across countries to become one of the dominant models, especially in countries where municipalities are responsible for WWS management (Marques, 2010).

Box 1.3. The regulatory framework for WWS in France

In France, municipalities have been responsible for drinking water services since 1789 and for sewerage services since 1992. Municipalities can operate WWS directly following a public management arrangement (called "*régie*") or they can delegate these services to a private operator under various delegated management arrangements. Regulation is carried out at the local level and the rights and obligations of both parties (e.g. the municipality and the water operator) are spelled out in the contract. The competition process "for" the market is supposed to make up for the absence of competition "in" the market and eliminate the market failures inherent to the provision of water and sanitation services. In addition, various *Services Déconcentrés de l'Etat* carry out a number of regulatory functions and supervise many aspects (financial, health, environmental) of contracts between municipalities and operators.

In 2007, this model of regulation was supplemented with the establishment of a national entity with specific regulatory powers, the French National Agency for Water and Aquatic Environment (ONEMA). Created by the 2006 law on water and aquatic environment, this national agency is in charge of preserving water quality and good ecological status of aquatic systems. As per its strategy, ONEMA has a four-fold mission: *i)* stimulate research and development; *ii)* manage the French Information System and produce data; *iii)* support territorial management of water and restoration of environments; and *iv)* protect aquatic environment by inspecting use and enforcing regulations. ONEMA works as a watchdog on water and sanitation services. However, being under the supervision of the Ministry of Environment, it does not benefit from legal and financial independence and its decisions are not legally binding.

Source: Marques (2010), *Regulation of Water and Wastewater services – An International Comparison*, IWA Publishing, London; ONEMA, www.onema.fr/ (accessed 1 April 2014).

In a third model, also called the "English model", the regulatory framework for WWS is organised around the establishment of dedicated agencies with regulatory functions. The dedicated water agency supervises and regulates the water sector independently from the private operators, the government and the consumers. This model allows separation of powers between the regulator and the line Ministers. This separation concentrates the regulatory functions into a single body and limits potential conflicts between policy formulation and enforcement. While it initially originated in the United Kingdom (see Box 1.4), this model has spread in other countries, including for instance recently to Italy.

Box 1.4. Regulating WWS through an independent agency: the case for the United Kingdom

In 1973, the adoption of the Water Act reduced drastically the number of entities operating WWS services to create 10 regional operators (Regional Water Authorities). These regional entities were dismantled in 1989 with the Water Act 1989 which initiated reform towards WWS privatisation. In the same year, OFWAT was created as the economic regulator for the water industry in England and Wales, the first of its kind in Europe, along with the environmental regulator (the Environment Agency) and with the drinking water quality regulator (the Drinking Water Inspectorate). OFWAT's statutory role and duties are primarily laid out in the Water Industry Act 1991. As the economic regulator, OFWAT is responsible for safeguarding WWS activities, protecting customer interests, guaranteeing the financial viability of companies, promoting economic efficiency and introducing competition. It regulates the tariff system, the quality of service for the water sector and it was recently given the power to impose penalties and sanctions.

Source: Marques (2010), *Regulation of Water and Wastewater services – An international comparison*, IWA Publishing, London.

These models are not mutually exclusive and increasingly, regulatory frameworks adopt features of the different models described above. For example, countries with contract agreements have not been prevented to create dedicated WWS regulatory agencies to supervise the quality of service and to intervene in case of conflicts (Marques, 2010). As highlighted in OECD (2007), "observations suggest that a broad continuum exists in terms of the regulatory models available – from the institutional to the contractual – and modes can also be combined".

The development of dedicated regulatory bodies for water services

The development of dedicated regulatory bodies for WWS stands out across countries as a response to some of the challenges of regulatory frameworks for water services. It has also accompanied the reform of the water industry that many countries have undergone over the past two decades – in particular the trend towards corporatisation of water operators (explicitly mentioned in the case of the Australian Capital Territory) and the consolidation of water service provision (in countries such as Ireland, Portugal and Ukraine for instance). In January 2008, a study conducted by Marques (2010) identified 136 water regulators spread over 57 countries worldwide: 12 in Africa, 5 in Asia, 16 in Europe, 2 in Oceania and 22 in America.

The OECD Survey on the Governance of Water Regulators carried out between September 2013 and September 2014 (Box 1.5) confirms this trend and shows the consistent emergence of dedicated regulatory bodies for water services over the past two decades.

Box 1.5. Background information on the OECD survey to water regulators

Thirty four regulators from 24 countries participated in the OECD survey on the Governance of Water Regulators (previously called the survey on Applying Better Regulation to the Water Sector). The list of respondents is provided in Annex A. They were selected on the basis that they were dedicated regulatory bodies established either as autonomous agencies or functionally separate entities within a ministry to carry out regulatory duties in relation to drinking water and sanitation services.

In Australia, Brazil and the United States (US), state level regulators (4, 1 and 6 respectively) contributed responses. For the United Kingdom, OFWAT from England and Wales, the Authority for Utility regulation of Northern Ireland and the Water Industry Commission for Scotland provided answers. In Belgium, the dedicated drinking water regulatory body embedded in the Flemish Environment Agency (VMM) participated. VMM is responsible only for the Flanders region and is dedicated to the regulation of the production and distribution of drinking water only. In Indonesia, the Jakarta Water Supply Regulatory Body is responsible for the Jakarta area only. In all other cases, the respondent has a nation-wide competence.

The sample of regulators covers a diverse group from different continents with various levels of income, environmental and institutional features. Out of the 34 regulators, 16 are located in Europe (12 in the European Union, the others mainly from Eastern Europe), 11 in America (6 in the US and 5 in South or Latin America), 2 in Asia (Indonesia and Malaysia), 4 in Oceania (Australia) and 1 in Africa (Mozambique). Out of the 23 countries represented by the survey answers, 10 are OECD Members (Australia, Belgium, Chile, Estonia, Hungary, Ireland, Italy, Portugal, United Kingdom, and United States), two are accession candidate countries (Colombia and Latvia) and two are Key Partners (Brazil and Indonesia).

Figure 1.1. **Year of operational establishment of water regulators**

(Number of regulators/34)

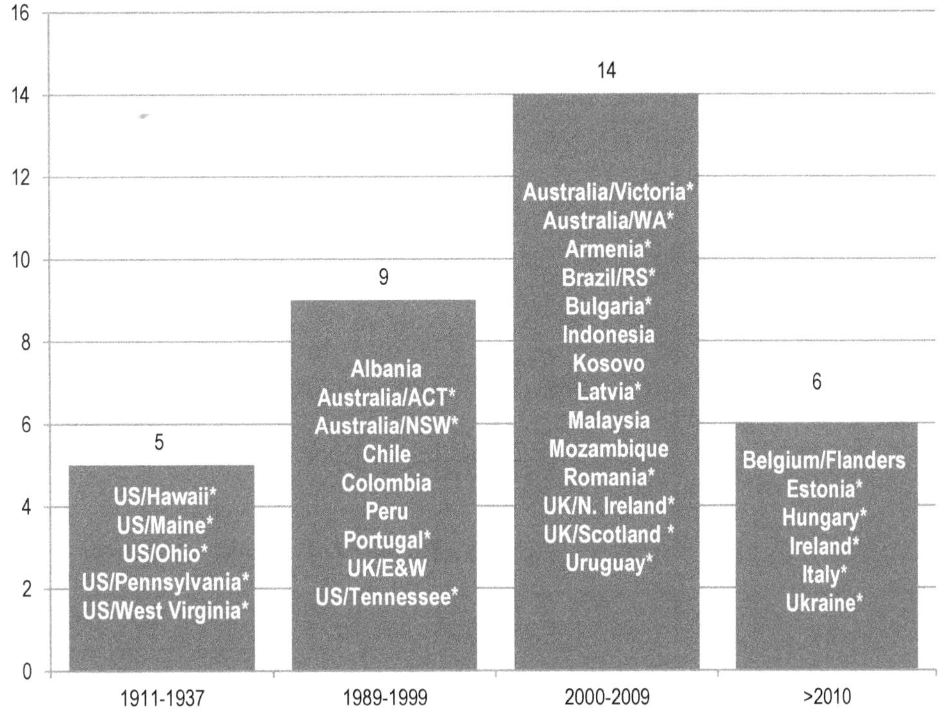

Note: * Multi-sector regulators.

Source: OECD Survey on the Governance of Water Regulators (2014).

Box 1.6. **Ongoing reforms in Jordan to establish an economic regulator for the water sector**

Jordan faces important shortcomings in the regulatory framework for water services. First, there is evidence of inappropriate enforcement of quality standards. Second, tariff regulation is a highly political endeavour and the approach remains ad hoc, as there is no established methodology for setting or revising tariff. Third, performance monitoring is not systematic and does not cover the overall sector. There are also challenges in relation to the quality of the information collected and the fragmentation of key performance indicators. Even when information is collected on water service provision, it is not made publically available.

In order to address these shortcomings, the government of Jordan has undertaken a number of reforms, including strengthening the role of the Project Management Unit (PMU) as the utility regulator within the Ministry of Water and Irrigation. New Rules of Procedure foresee that PMU performs a range of regulatory functions that are similar to the international experience, including; tariff regulation, monitoring of service delivery performance, analysis of business plans of utilities and information and data gathering. OECD (2014b) identifies the additional measures that Jordan will need to undertake to enable the transformation of the PMU into a credible economic regulator for the water sector. They involve improving clarity on PMU's roles and functions, aligning its resources with its core work and establishing appropriate accountability mechanisms to enhance the credibility of the regulatory framework. In parallel, the efforts to strengthen the autonomy of water providers need to be continued.

Source: OECD (2014b), *Water Governance in Jordan: Overcoming the Challenges to Private Sector Participation*, OECD Studies on Water, OECD Publishing, Paris, http://dx.doi.org/10.1787/9789264213753-en.

While North-American water regulators were established prior to 1939, most of the other water regulators who responded to the survey came into force between 1990 and 2009. Over the past four years, six additional water regulators became operational, mainly in Europe (Belgium/Flanders, Estonia, Italy, Hungary, Ireland and Ukraine) (Figure 1.1 above). The trend towards the establishment of water regulators continues to gain ground. This option is under consideration in a number of countries (including, but not limited to, Jordan as illustrated in Box 1.6 above).

Answers to the OECD survey also show a majority of multi-sector regulators. Twenty three regulators surveyed by the OECD are multi-sector. Water was part of the regulator's scope of activities from the beginning in 11 cases. In 12 cases, water was added afterwards. This is the case for Bulgaria, for instance, where water regulation was added to the portfolio of the Regulatory Agency for Energy in 2005, or of Italy where water was added to the portfolio of the energy regulator in 2012. In Ireland, the Commission for Energy Regulation (CER), established in 1999, added the water sector as part of its competencies under the Water Services (No. 1 and No. 2) Act of 2013. In Estonia, the Public Water and Supply and Sewerage Act of 2010 vested regulatory duties to the Competition Authority established in Oct 1993.

Figure 1.2. **Main reasons to justify the establishment of a water regulator**

(Number of regulators/33)

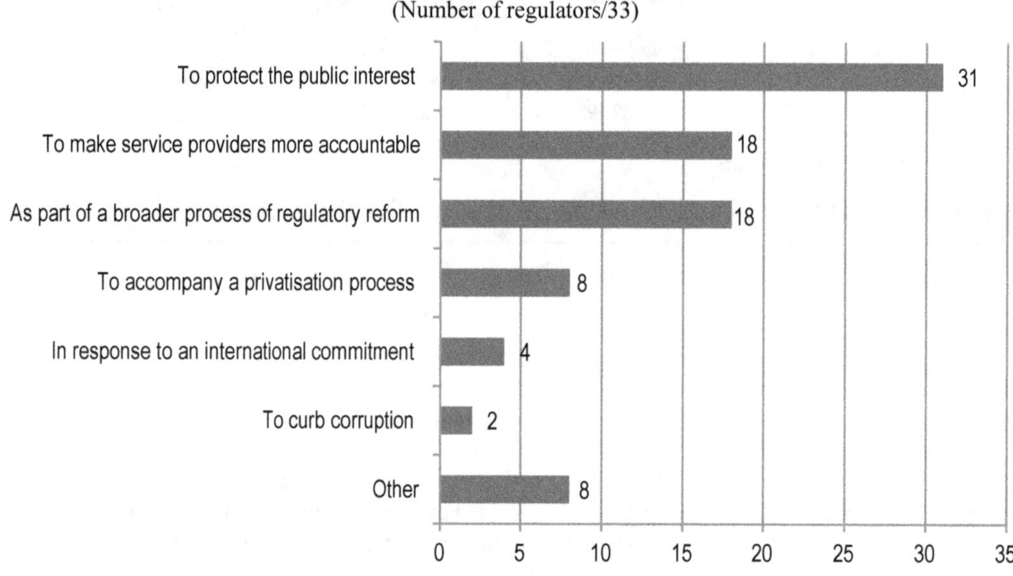

Note: The reasons for establishing the water regulator in Belgium/Flanders are unknown.

Source: OECD Survey on the Governance of Water Regulators (2014).

Of the 34 regulators who answered the OECD survey, the vast majority (31) justify the establishment of a regulator on the basis of protecting the public interest. This is by far the most frequently cited reason. Making the service providers more accountable and being part of a broader process of regulatory reform is next. It is often a combination of factors that justifies the establishment of a regulator, as illustrated by the fact that regulators provided several answers to the question and by the example of the statute of the National commission of the state public utilities of Ukraine (Box 1.7). In addition to the motivations already mentioned, regulators report the need to establish an independent price-setting process (explicitly mentioned by New South Wales in Australia for instance) or to harness regulatory expertise in the public sector (Colombia). Interestingly, "To accompany a privatisation process" is a reason for establishing a regulator provided in only one fourth of the cases. This is in line with the finding highlighted later on in the report that in a number of cases, the regulator has been established to oversee a fully public system.

Box 1.7. Establishing the National commission of the state public utilities in Ukraine

The reasons to create the National commission of the state public utilities regulation of Ukraine are clearly defined in its statute:

1. Balance interests of economic entities, consumers and the State
2. Ensure the transparency and openness of activity on the markets of natural monopolies and adjacent markets in the sphere of heat supply and centralised water supply and sewerage
3. Protect the rights of consumers, in particular, ensuring the provision of goods and services of proper quality and in sufficient amount at economically reasonable prices, and stimulating improvement of their quality and meeting the demand on them
4. Shape price and tariff policy and ensure its transparency for markets
5. Ensure the self-repayment of activity of subjects of natural monopolies and economic entities on adjacent markets
6. Provide equal possibilities for consumers to access goods (services) on markets, which are in the state of natural monopoly
7. Limit the influence of subjects of natural monopolies on state policy and stimulate competition on adjacent markets in the sphere of heat supply and centralised water supply and sewerage, recycling and disposal of waste to ensure the effective functioning of the respective spheres

Source: OECD Survey on the Governance of Water Regulators (2014).

Bibliography

Guerin-Schneider L., M. Nakhla, and A. Grand d'Esnon (2002), "Gestion et Organisation des services publics d'eau en Europe", Cahier No. 19, Cahiers de recherche – École des Mines de Paris, Centre de Gestion Scientifique, June.

Marques, R. (2010), *Regulation of Water and Wastewater Services – An International Comparison*, IWA Publishing, London.

Massarutto, A., L. Anwandter and E. Linares (2012), "Financial Economies of Scale in the Water Sector", Research Report, IEFE, Boconni University, www.iefe.unibocconi.it.

OECD (2014), *OECD Best Practice Principles for Regulatory Policy: The Governance of Regulators*, OECD Publishing, Paris, http://dx.doi.org/10.1787/9789264209015-en.

OECD (2014a), *Water Governance in the Netherlands: Fit for the Future?*, OECD Studies on Water, OECD Publishing, Paris, http://dx.doi.org/10.1787/9789264102637-en.

OECD (2014b), *Water Governance in Jordan: Overcoming the Challenges to Private Sector Participation*, OECD Studies on Water, OECD Publishing, Paris, http://dx.doi.org/10.1787/9789264213753-en.

OECD (2014c), *Water Governance in Tunisia: Overcoming the Challenges to Private Sector Participation*, OECD Studies on Water, OECD Publishing, Paris, DOI: http://dx.doi.org/10.1787/9789264174337-en.

OECD (2013), *Making Water Reform Happen in Mexico,* OECD Studies on Water, OECD Publishing, Paris, http://dx.doi.org/10.1787/9789264187894-en.

OECD (2012), "Recommendation of the Council on Regulatory Policy and Governance", www.oecd.org/gov/regulatory-policy/2012-recommendation.htm.

OECD (2011), *Water Governance in OECD countries: A multi-level approach*, OECD Publishing, Paris, http://dx.doi.org/10.1787/9789264119284-en.

OECD (2009), *Private Sector Participation in Water Infrastructure: OECD Checklist for Public Action*, OECD Studies on Water, OECD Publishing, Paris, http://dx.doi.org/10.1787/9789264059221-en.

OECD (2007), "The Regulation of Public Services in OECD Countries: An Overview of Water, Waste management and Public Transport", discussion paper, OECD, Paris.

Wackerbauer, J. (2009), "The Water Sector in Germany", *Working Paper*, CIRIEC No. 2009/11, November.

Chapter 2

Results of the OECD Survey on the Governance of Water Regulators

This chapter provides key insights into the governance of water regulators based on the answers provided by 34 regulators to the OECD survey. In particular, the Chapter describes for this sample of regulators their: 1) institutional setting; 2) mandates, roles and core regulatory functions; 3) internal organisation; 4) accountability mechanisms; 5) use of tools and mechanisms to ensure regulatory quality.

Institutional settings

Where they exist, water regulators are one entity in the, often, complex regulatory and policy framework for water services. Other public and non-governmental agencies play important roles that bear on the regulator's activities, including various ministries (e.g. health, local housing, the environment etc.); the legislature; sub-national authorities (state governments, municipalities etc.) and interest groups (e.g. consumer advocacy groups or association of utilities). The effectiveness of the regulator is therefore contingent on its ability to define its position in the institutional landscape and to co-ordinate its efforts with other relevant entities.

According to the OECD *Best Practice Principles for the Governance of Regulators*, "an effective regulator must have clear objectives, with clear and linked functions and the mechanisms to co-ordinate with other relevant bodies to achieve the desired regulator outcomes." In particular, this connotes:

1. Clear co-ordination mechanisms with other bodies (non-government and other levels of government) where this will assist in meeting their common objectives to reduce overlap and regulatory burden.
2. A founding legislation or other government tools to clarify the roles of the regulatory body so that the purpose of the regulator and the objectives of the regulatory scheme are clear to the regulator's staff, regulated entities and citizens.

In addition, as most regulators were established as dedicated regulatory bodies, this section analyses how "independence" or "autonomy" translates into the governance arrangements and operational modalities of regulators. The OECD *Best Practice Principles for the Governance of Regulators* underlines that "establishing the regulator with a degree of independence (both from those it regulates and from government) can provide greater confidence and trust that regulatory decisions are made with integrity". It also acknowledges that "there is no generally agreed definition of what characteristics make a regulator 'independent'". While it helps, "enshrining a regulator's independence in legislation does not guarantee that the regulator's behaviour and decisions will be independent. A culture of independence, strong leadership and an appropriate working relationship with government and other stakeholders are essential to independent regulatory behaviour". This section reviews what de facto conditions have been put in place in various contexts to preserve the autonomy of the water regulators.

The position of water regulators in the institutional landscape and co-ordination efforts with other relevant entities

The regulatory landscape

Across the countries and territories surveyed, regulators for WWS are part of a broader regulatory framework at national or sub-national level (Figure 2.1) that typically involves line ministries (environment or natural resources) in charge of water policies; ministries of finance, economy or public works responsible for investments in the sector, tax and public financial management; health department in charge of water quality standards; and ministries of environment in charge of effluents. Various public agencies also play a role in specific issues of water regulation. In particular, agencies in charge of environmental protection work in close co-ordination with the water regulator to monitor the environmental sustainability of the WWS services. Regulators also report competition authorities as having a role.

Local governments are also part of the institutional landscape for water regulation. In some cases, regulators report that municipalities are responsible for providing and managing water and wastewater service delivery (e.g. Armenia, Belgium/Flanders, Italy, Portugal, and Uruguay). In their scope of activity, local governments can be involved in WWS regulation. For instance, in Portugal, municipalities determine retail tariffs in collaboration with the water regulator as a shared competence.

Figure 2.1. **Water regulators in the institutional landscape**

National or State/Regional level

Government

Ministry of Environment
All but Mozambique

Ministry of Finance
Ex: Uruguay, Chile, Australia/NSW

Ministry of Transport and Infrastructure
Ex: Albania, Italy

Ministry of Housing
Ex: Bulgaria, Colombia, Indonesia, Romania, Ukraine,

Ministry/Department of Agriculture
Ex: US

Ministry of Health
All but Armenia, Estonia, Ireland, Portugal, UK/England & Wales, Uruguay

Ministry of Economic Development and Trade
Ex: Albania, Kosovo, Ukraine

Ministry of Economy
Ex: Bulgaria, Chile, Latvia, Uruguay

Ministry of public works
Ex: Belgium/Flanders, Bulgaria, Chile, Indonesia, Mozambique

Public agencies

Economic Water Regulator

Environmental agencies
Ex: Australia, Belgium, Scotland, Hungary, Ireland, Portugal, UK/England & Wales, US

Competition Authorities
Ex: Australia/ACT, Bulgaria, Portugal, UK/England & Wales, Ukraine

Other stakeholders

Ombudsman
Ex: Australia, Indonesia, UK/Scotland

Customer Association/Commission
Ex: Australia, Romania, UK/England & Wales, US

Water Association
Ex: Australia, Brazil, Bulgaria, Romania, US

Operators / Associations Operators
Ex: Australia, Bulgaria, Ireland, Italy, Kosovo, Portugal, UK/England & Wales, US

Association of regulatory agencies
Ex: Brazil/RGS, US

Local level

Municipalities and local authorities
Ex: Albania, Belgium/Flanders, Brazil/RGS, Bulgaria, Colombia, Estonia, Indonesia, Italy, Malaysia, Portugal

Operators

Source: OECD Survey on the Governance of Water Regulators (2014).

Co-ordination mechanisms

All regulators report some kind of co-ordination mechanisms to ensure close and effective dialogue with the different tiers of government involved in regulating water services. However, ad hoc arrangements seem to prevail over systematic and institutionalised mechanisms. For the vast majority of regulators (29 over 34), the legislation gives the regulator the capacity to share relevant and appropriate information with other bodies with shared objectives or shared competencies (Figure 2.2). The majority of regulators (28) de facto resort to *ad-hoc* meetings with the different levels of government regarding their fields of competences in water regulation as the main form of co-ordination (Figure 2.3). Fourteen regulators participate in regular meetings with all levels of government in charge of regulating water services. Some regulators hold regular meetings with regulators in other jurisdictions (e.g. Australia/New South Wales) and with other dedicated regulatory bodies (e.g. bi-monthly meetings between the water regulator and the other supervising bodies housed within the Flemish Environmental Agency; such as local water governance and wastewater supervisor).

Figure 2.2. **The legislative requirements for co-operation**

(Number of regulators/34)

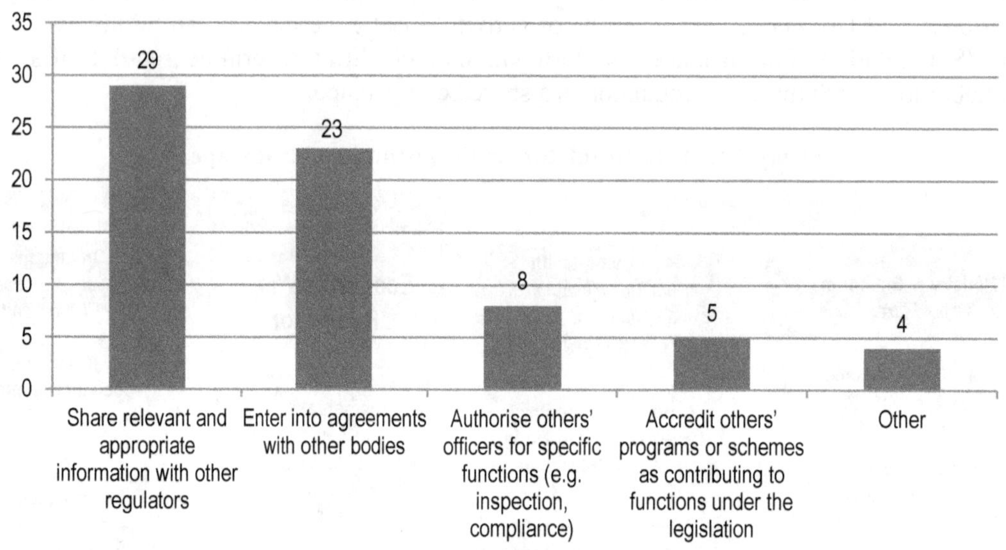

Source: OECD Survey on the Governance of Water Regulators (2014).

Figure 2.3. **Co-ordination mechanisms with all levels of government**

(Number of regulators/34)

	Number of regulators
There are ad hoc meetings on specific issues	28
There are agreements detailing respective roles and cooperation with regulators in other jurisdictions	14
There are regular meetings gathering all levels of government regulating water services	14
There is an electronic platform to share information among regulators	7
Other	7

Source: OECD Survey on the Governance of Water Regulators (2014).

Beyond exchange of information through meetings or else, typically the legislation grants the regulator the capacity to enter into agreements with other bodies in 23 cases, authorises others' officers for specific functions (e.g. inspection, compliance) in 8 cases, or accredits others' programs or schemes as contributing to functions under the legislation in 5 cases. A number of regulators (14) report having in place agreements detailing respective roles and co-operation with regulators in other jurisdictions. A handful of regulators have developed an electronic platform to share information among regulators (Uruguay, US/Maine, UK/Scotland, Kosovo, Colombia and Albania). In Portugal, co-ordination is guaranteed through the Advisory Council of ERSAR, which includes representatives of all levels of government to discuss the strategy and activities of the regulator.

The status of the regulatory body and its founding legislation

In line with the OECD *Best Practice Principles for the Governance of Regulators*, "the legislation that grants regulatory authority to a specific body should clearly state the objectives of the legislation and the powers of the authority. The objectives should be written in order to identify the ends to be achieved or the expected outcome, rather than specifying the means by which they will be achieved."

In line with the OECD principles, answers to the survey show that all the countries and territories surveyed have adopted a specific legislation to establish the regulatory body for water services and to determine its role and responsibilities, rather than a decree unless this one complemented an existing law (e.g. Indonesia and Ukraine). In addition, all countries and territories define the duties of the regulators in law (for the specific case of Indonesia in a Decree). Box 2.1 provides the example of the legislation establishing the Energy and Water Regulatory Commission as the regulator for WSS in Bulgaria.

Box 2.1. **Legislation establishing the Water Regulatory Commission in Bulgaria**

In 2005, the State Energy Regulatory Commission of Bulgaria expanded its scope of activity to cover water supply and sewerage services. The Law on Regulation of WWS services (SG, No. 18 of 25.02.2005, last amended in 2013: SG No. 103/29.11.2013) amended the Law on Energy Sector (SG 107 from 9.12.2003) to establish the State Energy and Water Regulatory Commission (SEWRC) and define its statutes. The seven chapters of the law (The Law on Regulation of WWS services) establish the legal framework for the regulation of prices, accessibility and quality of water-supply and sewerage services.

- Provisions related to the establishment of the legal framework for the regulation of prices, accessibility and quality of water-supply and sewerage services (Chapter 1 – General dispositions);
- Provisions establishing that the water-supply and sewerage services shall be regulated by the State Energy and Water Regulatory Commission, its powers and sources of revenues (Chapter 2 – Regulation of water-supply and sewerage services);
- Provisions specifying how the Commission should measure and assess the quality of the water-supply and sewerage services and approve the business-plans prepared by utilities (Chapter 3 – Regulation of water supply and sewerage service quality);
- Provisions defining how the Commission should regulate prices (Chapter 4 – Water-supply and sewerage service price regulation);

Box 2.1. **Legislation establishing the Water Regulatory Commission in Bulgaria** (*cont.*)

- Provisions detailing how the Commission should exercise control on the utilities (Chapter 5 – Control);
- Provisions providing for the establishment of a National Information System on Water-Supply and Sewerage Services by the Commission (Chapter 6 – Information System); and
- Provisions detailing the penalties that the Commission can impose on the utilities (Chapter 7 – Administrative Penalty Provisions).

Source: Water Supply and Sewerage Services Regulation Act, www.dker.bg/docsen.php?d=98.

Level of autonomy across various dimensions (political, administrative and financial)

The majority of regulators in the survey can be defined as independent regulatory body (Figure 2.4). Exceptions include Romania, where the regulator is an authority subordinated to a minister. In Belgium/Flanders the regulator is a sub-entity of a Governmental agency and has mainly an advisory role. In the case of Indonesia the regulatory body is independent but has a pure advisory capacity. In Estonia, the regulatory duties for WWS have been vested to the competition authority.

Figure 2.4. **Status of the regulatory agency**

(Number of regulators/34)

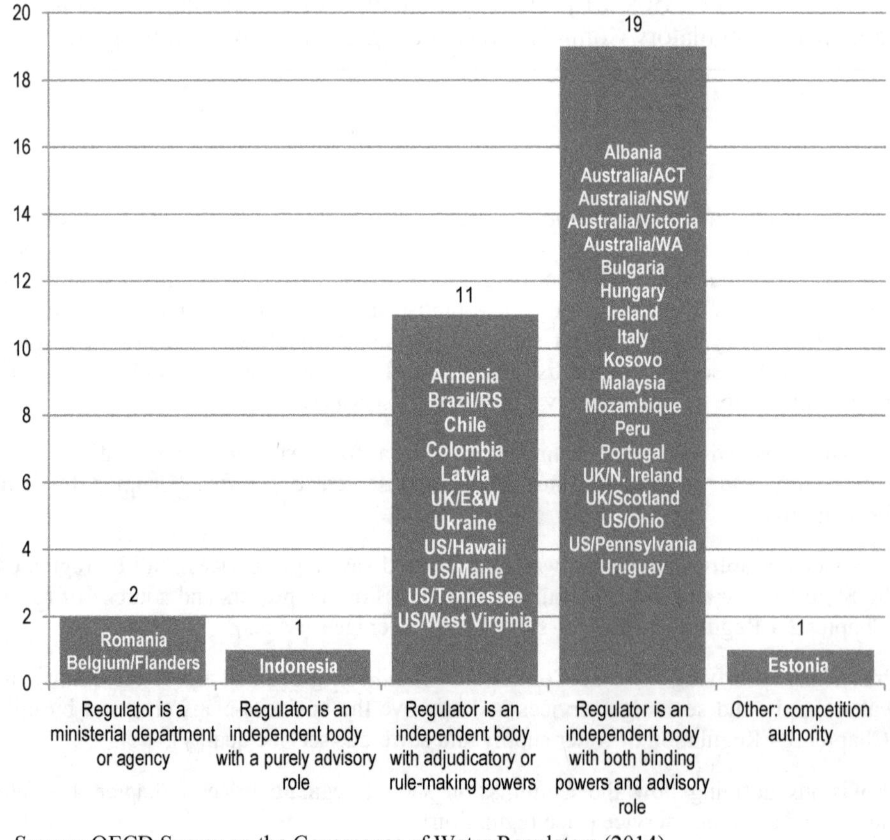

Source: OECD Survey on the Governance of Water Regulators (2014).

De jure independence through explicit reference in the law is achieved for 22 regulators (Figure 2.5). *De facto* independence of regulators is ensured through a mix of governance features and operational modalities. These involve independent decision making, i.e. decisions that are taken without being subject to government assessment (28 regulators); staffing based on technical grounds rather than political criteria (28 regulators); protection of the board and top management from political interferences (26 regulators); and a budget which does not depend primarily on the government (23 regulators). In 13 cases, the regulator combines both *de jure* and all *de facto* conditions, achieving, at least on paper, the organisation most likely to ensure independence (Figure 2.6). It is also noteworthy that although formally a sub-entity of a governmental agency, Belgium/Flanders enjoys some degree of autonomy, in particular in relation to the top management (which cannot be removed based on political decisions) and technical staff (who is chosen on technical ground and not based on political criteria).

Figure 2.5. **Ensuring independence from political influence**

(Number of regulators/33)

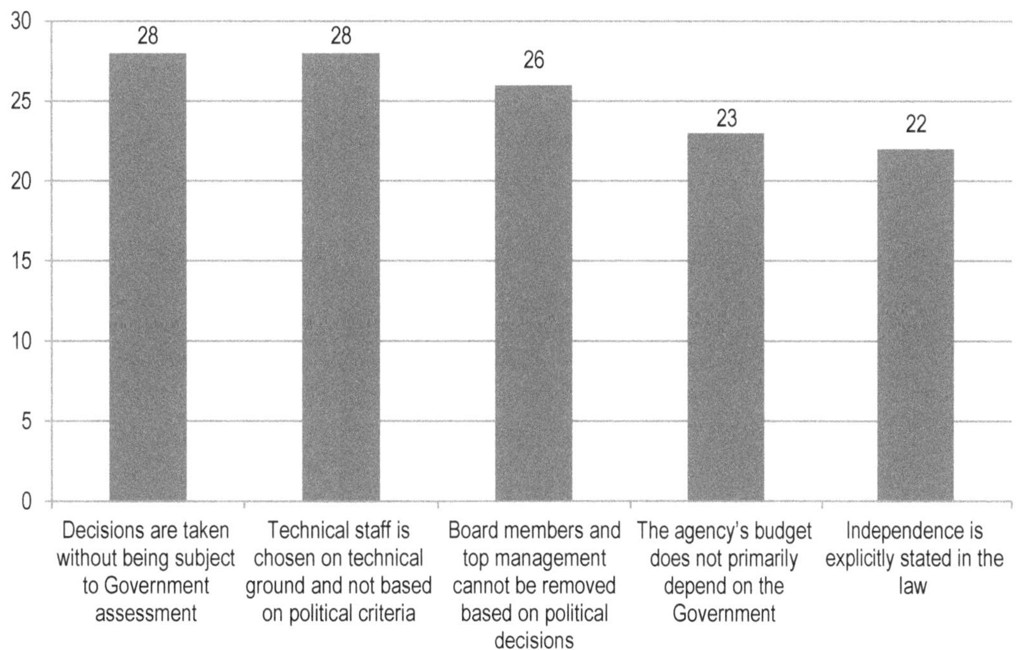

Note: The figure excludes Romania.

Source: OECD Survey on the Governance of Water Regulators (2014).

The *OECD Best Practice Principles for Regulatory Policy: The Governance of Regulators* acknowledges that the value of independence situates the regulator at "arm's length" from government and defines it to mean that "the regulator is not subject to the direction on individual regulatory decisions by executive government". However, they also establish that "all regulators should operate within the power delegated by the legislature and remain subject to long term national policy". The survey to water regulators has therefore sought to complement the information on independence of decision making of water regulators by identifying when the regulators can receive instructions or official guidance from the government or the parliament, whether the regulator needs to submit proposals for new regulation to other bodies for approval and whether its decisions can be overturned.

Figure 2.6. **Number of *de jure* and *de facto* conditions to ensure independence**

(Number of regulators/33)

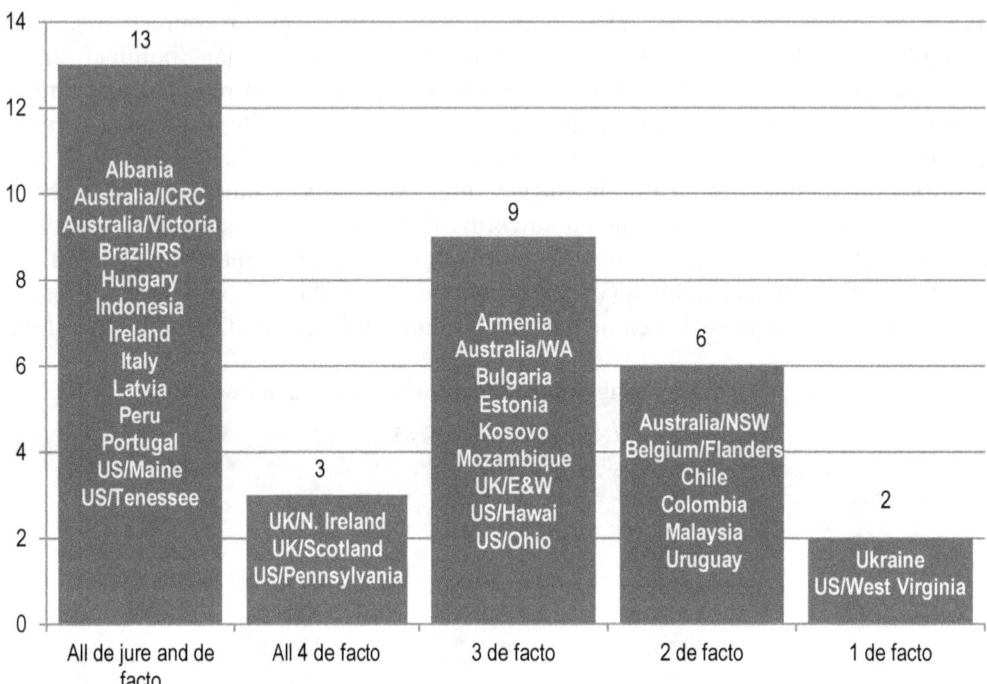

Note: The figure excludes Romania.

Source: OECD Survey on the Governance of Water Regulators (2014).

Figure 2.7. **Can the regulator receive instructions or official guidance from the government or the parliament?**

(Number of regulators/34)

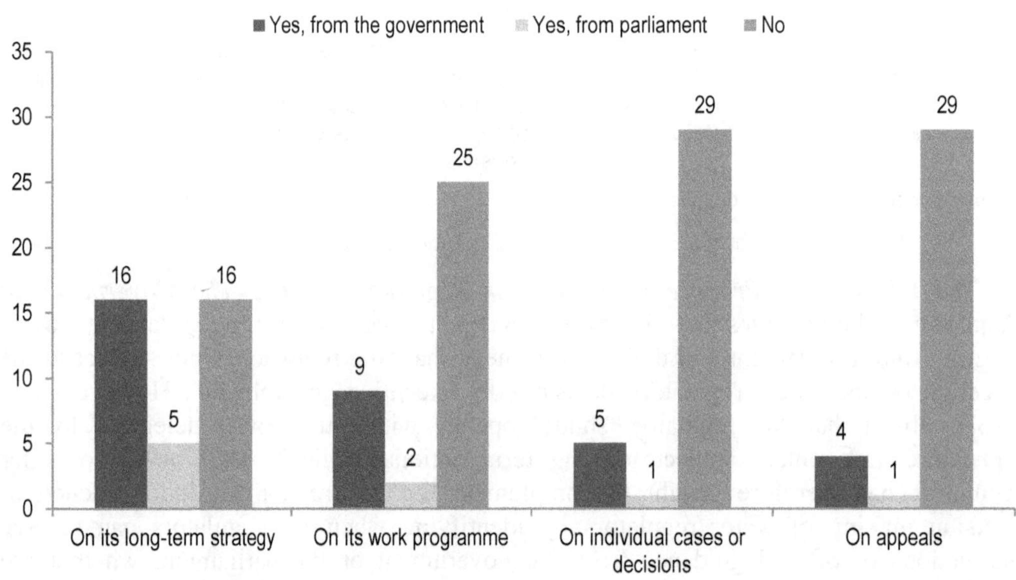

Source: OECD Survey on the Governance of Water Regulators (2014).

Sixteen regulators report receiving instructions or official guidance from the government on their long-term strategy and five receive them from the parliament (Figure 2.7). Overall, 18 regulators receive instructions or official guidance on their long-term strategy, either from the government or from parliament, which is consistent with it being subject to the national policy. In three cases, both the government and the parliament can provide this guidance. In nine cases, the regulator is subject to this influence directly in relation to its work programme, which may reflect a more direct interference in the operations of the regulator but may also remain at a higher policy level. In five cases (Australia/New South Wales, Belgium/Flanders, Kosovo, Malaysia and UK/Northern Ireland), the intervention takes place on individual cases and decisions and in four other cases (Malaysia, Mozambique, US/Ohio and US/Pennsylvania), the intervention takes place on appeals.

In Australia/New South Wales, while IPART has statutory powers to make price determinations under the *Independent Pricing and Regulatory Tribunal Act*, the relevant Minister can issue a direction notice to IPART. In UK/Northern Ireland, the regulator is issued a Social and Environmental Guidance at each price control in the water sector (it does not apply to the energy sector) and has a legal "duty to have regard to" such advice. The advice can contain government steers, wishes as well as specific targets and/or requirements to comply with EU directives.

Half of the regulators enjoy important autonomy in their regulatory activities and do not need to submit proposals for new regulation to other bodies for approval. Generally, the level of autonomy of the regulators depends on the regulatory matter at hand. For instance, in Australia/New South Wales, IPART is both fully autonomous in determining the prices for public water utilities and subject to governmental or ministerial approval on decisions such as licensing (e.g. the Minister may choose not to adopt IPART's recommendations as to whether a private water utility should be granted a licence). In US/West Virginia, certain rulemakings need to be submitted to State legislator. In Uruguay, the regulator needs approval to develop higher-rank norms, but not to develop technical regulation.

In 22 cases, no body (other than a court) can overturn the decisions of the regulator. In some cases, a specialised body can overturn the decisions of the regulator. This is for instance the case in England and Wales where the Competition and Markets Authority can intervene for price control determinations and licence modifications. In Chile, the General Comptroller of the Republic can intervene, but only to statute about illegality.

The survey was an opportunity to gather qualitative information about how selected regulators perceive their independence and protection against external influence (Table 2.1).

Table 2.1. **Selected responses to the survey question: "Does legislation foresee any mechanism to ensure that regulatory decisions are protected from capture by political or private interests?"**

Australia/New South Wales	The IPART Act requires Tribunal members to disclose any pecuniary interests. If a Tribunal makes such a disclosure, that Tribunal member must then not be present during any relevant deliberation of the Tribunal or take part in making a relevant determination.
UK/England and Wales	Our independence from ministers and rules of procedure protect against external influence.
Italy	Independence of the Regulator as stated in law (i.e. nomination criteria, decision powers, self-organization provisions, finance and budget, accountability appeal of decisions rules).

Table 2.1. **Selected responses to the survey question: "Does legislation foresee any mechanism to ensure that regulatory decisions are protected from capture by political or private interests?"** (*cont.*)

Peru	The law establishes the regulator as an independent and technical body. In addition, the Board members are prohibited from having personal investments in utilities and from having professional connection directly or indirectly with any utility under the scope of the Regulator.
Portugal	The public disclosure of information enables the stakeholders to appeal against a presumable harmful decision taken due to capture by political or private interests.
US/Maine	*Ex parte* communications are prohibited. Commissioner personnel are prohibited from having personal investments in public utilities, and may not have a professional connection with any public utility or be a member of a firm that renders provides services to a public utility.
UK/Scotland	It is the role of the Competition Authority to ensure protection against capture.
Malaysia	The regulator was established as an independent corporate body and may be sued in its own name.
Uruguay	The staff may not work for or have any relation with regulated companies, and also the Members of the board may not run for office in the next election.
US/Hawaii, Ohio, Pennsylvania	Ethics and conflict of interest reporting.

Source: OECD Survey on the Governance of Water Regulators (2014).

Mandate and roles

The OECD *Best Practice Principles for the Good Governance of Regulators* identifies role clarity as essential for a regulator to understand and fulfil its objectives effectively. This requires that the regulator's objectives, functions and scope of activities are clearly defined and communicated to all stakeholders and that duplication of tasks and mandates with other public institutions are avoided. "The overview of water regulatory frameworks in OECD" shows that there is a wide range of functions to be performed in relation to water services and that the governance arrangements presiding to the *de jure* or *de facto* allocation of these functions vary greatly across countries (including the specific role of dedicated regulatory bodies). Allocation of these functions may also evolve over time as reforms in the WWS sector take place. This section seeks to identify the main responsibilities of water regulators across the sample. The success of the regulator in undertaking its functions will depend on the breadth and depth of the powers granted by legislation and other defining texts and practices. The review of regulatory functions is complemented by an analysis of the powers of the regulator in practice.

The competencies of regulators

Two-thirds of the regulators surveyed (23 regulators) are multi-sector bodies (Figure 2.8). For the majority of multi-sector regulators (20 out of 23), water is bundled with energy competencies (electricity and gas). Other combinations involve transport, telecommunications, solid waste management, and district heating. Regulatory bodies from Eastern Europe – in particular the Public Utilities Commission (PUC) of Latvia, the Energy and Public Utility Regulatory Authority of Hungary, the National Authority for Public Utilities (NAPU) of Romania, as well as some of the US state regulators stand out in terms of number of sectors covered. PUC in Latvia for instance performs regulatory functions in relation to energy, electronic communications, post, railway transport, waste disposal and water management. NAPU in Romania regulates water supply; sewerage and purification used waters; sewerage and evacuation of pluvial waters; production, transportation, distribution and supply of thermal energy in a centralised system; sanitation of towns; public lighting; and local public transportation, among others.

Figure 2.8. **Competencies of regulators**

(Number of regulators/34)

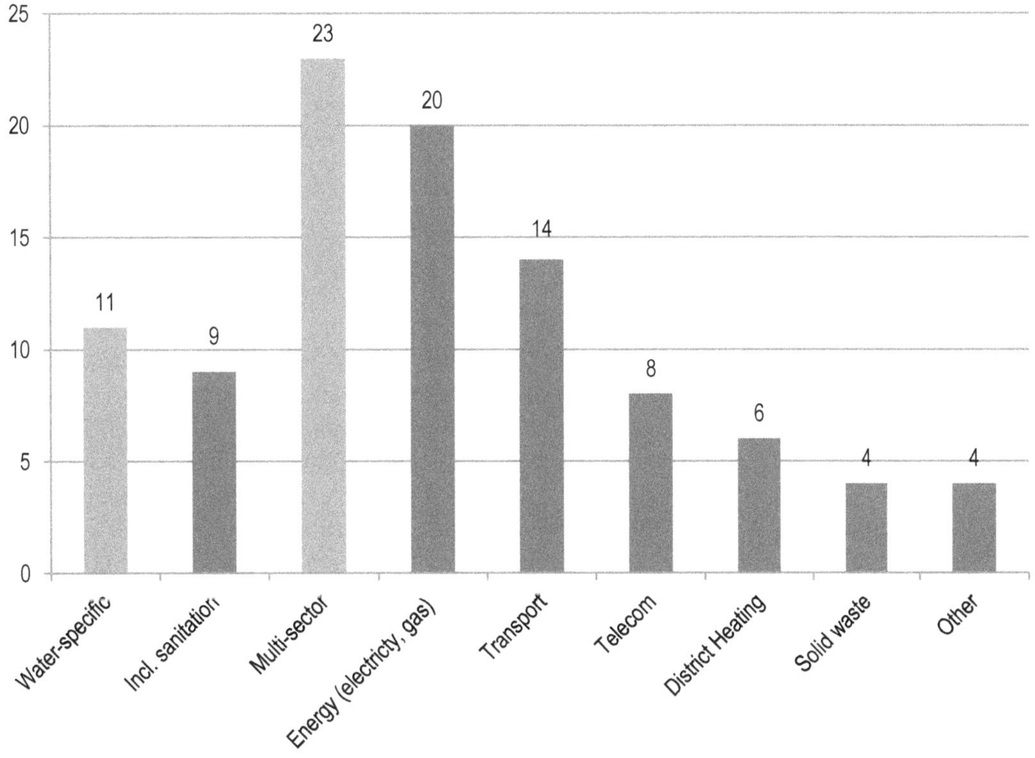

25
20
15
10
5
0
23
20
14
11
9
8
6
4
4
Water-specific
Incl. sanitation
Multi-sector
Energy (electricty, gas)
Transport
Telecom
District Heating
Solid waste
Other

Source: OECD Survey on the Governance of Water Regulators (2014).

For most of the multi-sector regulators (19 out of 23), the administrative and support services are joint, allowing some economies of scale and synergies between the different sectors. In a number of cases (including Australia/New South Wales, Bulgaria, Ukraine), the fact that water shares the features of a monopolistic sector with other sectors is an important driver for making linkages across and in particular for experience sharing. The bundling of responsibilities and competences strengthens the position of the regulator and provides it with increased authority to deal with dominant position. In 9 cases, regulators report that the sectors in their portfolio have different business cycles, which allow the technical staff to work transversally.

It is worth noting that in half of the cases, the establishment of a multi-sector regulator was motivated by an evaluation of the benefits and challenges of bundling several sectors together. In two instances (Bulgaria and Latvia), the case was supported by work by the World Bank. In Latvia, an analysis carried out by the regulator describes the advantages of multi-sector regulation (Box 2.2).

Box 2.2. Latvia: the advantages of multi-sector regulation

- Uniform regulatory strategy and similar approaches in all regulated sectors;
- Similar procedures in dealing with customer complaints, supervision of utilities;
- Ability to apply experience from one sector to other sector;
- Multi-sector model increases independence – no sector dominates the agenda, no financial dependence on any sector or large utility; and
- Better use of expertise and resources, especially important for a small country.

Source: Karnitis, E. and A. Virtmanis (2011), "Multi-sectoral regulation of services of general economic interest: Ten-year experience of Latvia", Public Utilities Commission of Latvia, Riga, www.sprk.gov.lv/uploads/doc/Multiregulator.pdf.

Role clarity

In all 34 cases, objectives and mission of the regulator are specified in legislation. In six cases, three US states, Portugal, UK/Northern Ireland and UK/Scotland, the line minister provided in addition a statement of expectations to the regulator. In UK/England and Wales, the Department for Environment, Food and Rural Affairs (DEFRA) issued in May 2013 a strategic policy statement to OFWAT.[1] Other mechanisms to clarify expectations *vis-à-vis* the regulator, as reported in the survey, include specific and monitored agreements between the line ministry and the regulator. In Chile, for instance, the regulator carries out its activities under a three-year performance agreement with annual evaluation by the Ministry of Public Works. In Belgium/Flanders, the activities of the regulatory body are part of a policy agreement between the Flemish Environment Agency (VMM) and the Ministry of Environment, which includes performance indicators. The implementation of the agreement is the object of an annual report/evaluation.

Scope of activity and market structure

The structure of the water industry differs greatly across countries (Figure 2.9). In some territories, one or a handful of big companies are responsible for the bulk of water service provision. This is for instance the case in Australia/Capital Territory, Ireland, UK/Northern Ireland and UK/Scotland, where there is only one household supplier. In some cases, the consolidation of the water industry is very recent or still on-going (see the example of Ireland in Box 2.3). In other territories, the water industry is fragmented. This is the case in Romania (1 043 operators for a population of 20 million), Ukraine (1 595 operators for a population of 45.5 million), Italy (2 000 operators for a population of 59.5 million), US/Pennsylvania (2 100 operators for a population of 12.8 million) and Colombia (2 500 operators for a population of 46.6 million).

Figure 2.9. **Number of active water operators in the water and sewerage sector**

(Number of regulators/33)

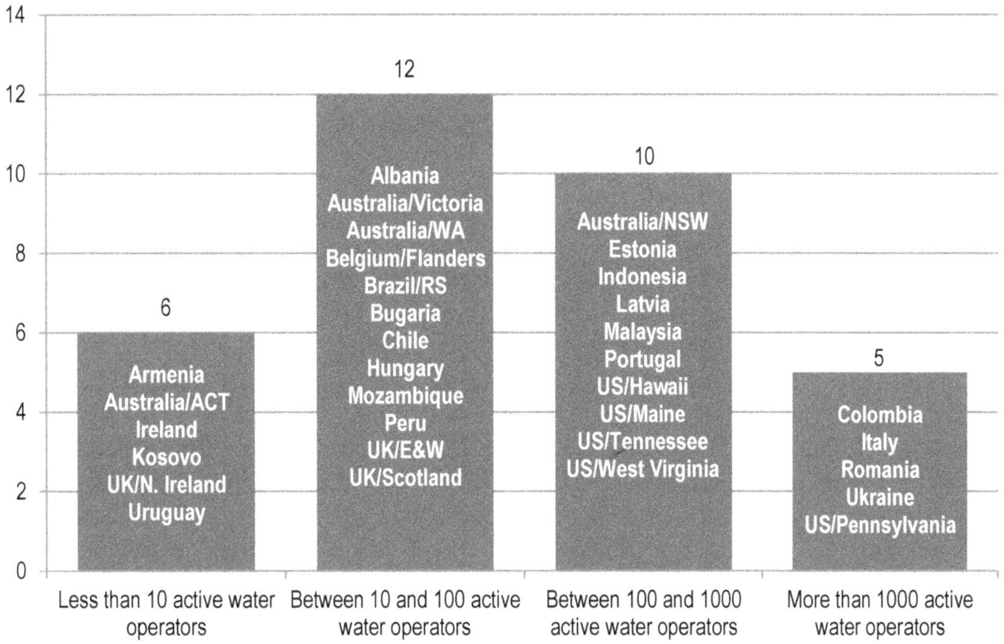

Less than 10 active water operators	Between 10 and 100 active water operators	Between 100 and 1000 active water operators	More than 1000 active water operators
6	12	10	5
Armenia Australia/ACT Ireland Kosovo UK/N. Ireland Uruguay	Albania Australia/Victoria Australia/WA Belgium/Flanders Brazil/RS Bugaria Chile Hungary Mozambique Peru UK/E&W UK/Scotland	Australia/NSW Estonia Indonesia Latvia Malaysia Portugal US/Hawaii US/Maine US/Tennessee US/West Virginia	Colombia Italy Romania Ukraine US/Pennsylvania

Notes: Excluding US/Ohio. In Belgium/Flanders, the number of active operators is less than 10 from 1 January 2015 onwards.

Source: OECD Survey on Applying Better Regulation in the Water Service Sector (2014).

Box 2.3. **Consolidation of the water industry in Ireland**

Irish Water is Ireland's new national water utility that is responsible for providing and developing water services throughout Ireland. Incorporated in July 2013, as a semi-state company under the Water Services Act 2013, Irish Water has brought the water and wastewater services of the 34 local authorities together under one national service provider. Irish Water will gradually take over the responsibilities from these local authorities on a phased basis from January 2014. It will take approximately five years for Irish Water to be fully established, at which point it will be responsible for the operation of public water services including management of national water assets, maintenance of the water system, investment and planning, managing capital projects and customer care and billing. As well as responsibility for public water services, Irish Water will also be making capital and investment decisions regarding the country's water infrastructure on a national basis. Irish Water is accountable to two regulatory bodies – the Commission for Energy Regulation (CER), the economic regulator for the water industry, and the Environmental Protection Agency (EPA), the environmental regulator.

Source: www.water.ie/about-us/company/about-irish-water/.

In 24 cases, the water regulator is responsible for all water operators active in the jurisdiction. In a few cases, however, the regulator manages a small share of the number of water operators although those may be large operators. In Ukraine, for instance, according to the latest annual report of the National Commission of the State Public

Utilities Regulation of Ukraine (2013), 1 595 water operators are active in the water and wastewater sector. The regulator has responsibility for 150 of them (i.e. 9.4% of the total). However, together, they cover 92% of the total water supply and water services. In Australia/New South Wales, IPART regulates 20 of the 123 public and private water providers, e.g. some 16% – the remaining entities are regional water utilities regulated by the Office of Water, a governmental department. However, together these 20 providers account for some 78% of the industry turnover. In Mozambique, the regulator oversees all 15 companies present in the formal urban sector. However, more than 500 informal small operators are reportedly active in the sector, falling outside of the scope of activity of the water regulator.

For two thirds of the sample (22 regulators), the regulator supervises both private entities and state-owned utilities. The exceptions involve cases in some US states (Hawaii, Ohio, and Pennsylvania) and in Indonesia, where the regulator has a specific responsibility to supervise private sector entities. By contrast, in several cases, the regulator has been established to supervise a fully public system – it is the case of Australia/Victoria, Belgium/Flanders and UK/Northern Ireland for instance. The condition, clearly specified in the case of Latvia, is that the public entities under supervision have an enterprise status (Government agencies are supervised by local governments).

Most regulators in the sample mainly oversee urban activities and centralised systems over a certain size. In several cases – Australia/Capital Territory, Chile, Indonesia, Mozambique and Peru – the regulator does not have prerogative for rural water. In Indonesia, the regulator has a specific competence for the Jakarta area. In Peru, the regulator has responsibility for urban cities above 15 000 inhabitants. In Ukraine, the Commission regulates entities which provide centralised water supply and sewerage services in one or more settlements in urban and rural areas within one region with a population of not less than 30 000 inhabitants and volumes of more than 300 000 m^3/year of water supply; and 200 000 m^3/year of sewerage. In Estonia, the water companies who operate in territory with a population of 2 000 or more are under the control of the Competition Authority for the regulation of prices and connection fees. The remaining companies are regulated by the local governments.

While there is no optimal number of regulated entities, the impact of the market structure in terms of balance of powers between the industry and the regulator is non-negligible – the fewer the number of regulated entities and the bigger their size, the greater will be their bargaining power. Consequently, the market structure will influence the functions and powers of the regulator. In the case of a consolidated industry, the regulator needs to be embedded with substantial enforcement powers (UK/England and Wales). In the case of fragmented water industry, it is likely that the regulator will have a strong capacity building role (Portugal).

Core regulatory functions and powers

Based on the answers to the questionnaire, the core functions and powers of the majority of water regulators can be structured around 4 areas (figures 1.10 and 1.11):

- Economic regulation (tariff setting and review of utilities' investment plans);
- Data collection and performance monitoring related to water services;
- Enforcement of regulations and standards; and

- Customer engagement and protection.

By contrast, activities related to quality standards for drinking water or for wastewater treatment are for the majority of water regulators outside of the scope of their responsibilities. Quality standards for drinking water usually fall within the remit of ministries of health or environmental protection agencies. Quality standards for wastewater are usually within the responsibility of the environment ministries. Where the regulator has a role, it is generally in relation to the enforcement of the quality standards. This is for instance the case in Australia/NSW or in Chile. Similarly, the definition of public service obligation is within the purview of the government, as part of its general policy making. Promoting demand management and defining industry standards are usually competencies that are shared with the operators.

Figure 2.10. **Core regulatory functions carried out by the regulators**

(Number of regulators/34)

	Yes	No
Tariff regulation	33	1
Monitoring of service delivery performance	32	2
Information and data gathering	27	7
Analysing utilities' investment/business plans	27	7
Customer engagement	25	9
Consumer protection and dispute resolution	25	9
Incentives for efficient investment	24	10
Defining technical & service standards	22	12
Incentives for efficient use of water resources	22	12
Uniform systems of accounts	20	14
Promoting demand management	20	14
Promoting innovative technologies	18	16
Licensing of water operators	17	17
Carrying management audits on utilities	16	18
Defining public service obligations	15	19
Supervision of contracts with private actors	14	20
Supervising utilities' financing activities	11	23
Quality standards for drinking water	9	25
Quality standards for wastewater treatment	4	30

Source: OECD Survey on the Governance of Water Regulators (2014).

Figure 2.11. **Core powers of the regulators**

(Number of regulators/34)

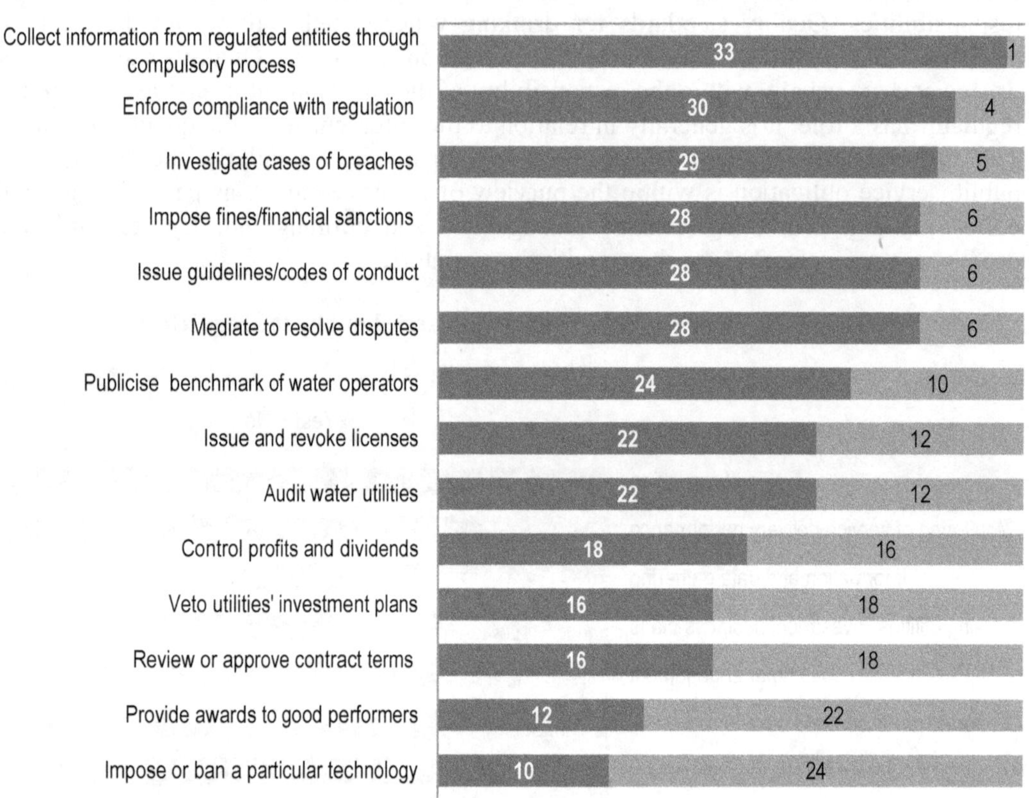

Source: OECD Survey on the Governance of Water Regulators (2014).

Economic regulation

All the regulators surveyed except one have responsibility for tariff regulation (in Australia/Western Australia, the state government retains the price-setting function for water service providers). In a number of cases, this responsibility is mainly carried out in an advisory role (for instance in Belgium/Flanders, Hungary, Indonesia and Uruguay). Among the 29 regulators with statutory powers in relation to tariff setting, 20 regulators report carrying this function by reference to a particular methodology or criteria defined by law. In 9 cases, the regulator has discretion in determining the tariffs and the methodology – although in a number of cases, the regulator carries out this function within a general frame set by the law (Mozambique, Uruguay), and in reference to certain criteria (Australia/Capital Territory).

Methodologies differ substantially across regulators at least in their details (Annex B gathers the information provided by regulators on tariff methodologies in response to the OECD survey). Overall, however, cost-plus approaches are the most widely used. Several regulators have elaborated the cost-plus approach by taking into account performance achievement in the consideration of costs (Albania, Kosovo and Mozambique). A number of regulators are in the process of transitioning away from the cost-plus approach to a new tariff setting methodology. Bulgaria for instance has moved from a rate of return approach in 2006-08 to a price cap approach in 2009-2013. Malaysia is also considering a new tariff setting approach.

Availability of information on various dimensions of the utilities' operations (including costs and investments) is critical to support appropriate tariff setting. In line with this principle, 27 regulators are responsible for analysing the investment or the business plan of the utilities and 22 regulators have the power to audit utilities, which is likely to provide the background information for appropriate tariff setting. However, in six cases, while the regulator has responsibility for tariff setting, it does not have the responsibility of analysing the investment or the business plan of the utilities, which may generate some asymmetry of information.

Monitoring of service performance

The second most frequent function carried out by regulators is related to the monitoring of service delivery performance (32 of the 34 regulators). The exceptions include Colombia and Estonia, where this responsibility is vested to a different authority (respectively the Superintendence of Public Service, and local authorities). In 27 cases, this function is combined with the function of information and data gathering. The critical importance of this function for water regulators is reflected in the allocation of powers to the regulators. The most consistent power across water regulators consists in collecting information from regulated entities through compulsory processes (33 regulators). The exception is Colombia, where it is carried out by the Superintendence of Public Service. This confirms the main reasons for establishing the regulator in the first place, i.e. protecting the public interest, and improving transparency of information and accountability of the water service sector. It positions water regulators as critical players in the reforms towards more transparency and a user-centric approach.

However, while disclosure is a critical dimension that provides legitimacy and credibility to data collection, it remains to be achieved in a number of countries. Responses to the survey show that a small number of regulators do not make the performance information that they collect (e.g. about the service provided, costs, quality) publicly available. This is the case for instance in Hungary, Latvia, Malaysia and in a number of US states. In a number of countries, the information is only partially available (Belgium/Flanders and Uruguay for instance). Reasons invoked include for instance the confidentiality of information (in particular of financial information). In the case of Belgium/Flanders, 'confidentiality' has been agreed upon in a protocol between the regulator and the water suppliers. Mostly, this leads the regulator to publish consolidated information but not the detailed breakdown.

Twenty four regulators have the power to publicise benchmarks for water operators – even though in some cases, it may not be done yet (Ireland and Malaysia). The benchmarking exercises remain highly heterogeneous across regulators, both in terms of the scope and nature of the performance indicators used and in terms of the reference points. As an example, Annex C provides the performance indicators collected by the regulators in Bulgaria, Peru, Portugal and UK/England and Wales. In most cases, operators within a country or a jurisdiction are compared with each other. In the case where there is only one or very few active operators in the market, benchmarking can be carried out against their own targets (e.g. Scottish Water)[2] or against international experience (it is planned that Irish Water would be benchmarked against comparable water operators abroad, including Scottish Water, Northern Ireland and English/Welsh operators). This however requires that similar characteristics of the water sector can be found elsewhere.

Regulatory enforcement

Regulators consistently have strong enforcement roles and powers. They constitute a critical link in the regulatory governance cycle, towards the concrete implementation of government policies. Most regulators can enforce compliance with regulation (30), investigate cases of breaches (29), and issue codes of conduct and guidelines (28) either independently or together with other bodies. Twenty eight regulators have the power to impose fines and financial sanctions to operators in case of regulatory infringements. Twenty two can issue and revoke licences.

In four cases, the regulator has neither the power to investigate cases of breaches, nor to impose sanctions (Armenia, Colombia, Indonesia, and Ireland). Although in the case of Ireland, the regulator has entered in a voluntary agreement with the operator whereby the regulator may require the operator to pay a penalty up to EUR 100 to customers where it breaches its code of practice. In two cases (Malaysia and UK/Scotland), the regulator has the power to investigate cases of breaches but not to impose a sanction. In Malaysia, while the regulator is given the power to investigate cases of breaches, the power to impose fines and imprisonment on breaches of the law lies with the courts. The regulator develops investigation papers that are submitted to the Deputy Public Prosecutor for a direction as to whether the case is to be filed in court. In cases of breaches of the licensing conditions by the service providers, the regulator can recommend to the minister to revoke the licence.

Table 2.2. **Examples of sanctions**

Type of sanctions	Territories
Monetary penalties	Albania Australia/New South Wales Belgium/Flanders Brazil/Rio Grande do Sul Bulgaria Kosovo Hungary Italy Latvia Malaysia Peru Portugal UK/England and Wales Ukraine United States/West Virginia
Revoking licences/operating certificates	Chile Hungary Latvia Malaysia United States/Tennessee
Warnings	Brazil/Rio Grande do Sul Italy Latvia Portugal
Audits	Italy Portugal United States/Tennessee
Requirements to act/Orders requiring compliance	Portugal UK/England and Wales United-States/Maine
Imprisonment	Malaysia
Imposing lower ROE	United-States/Hawaii, Ohio & Pennsylvania
Subsequent reporting	United-States/Maine

Source: OECD Survey on the Governance of Water Regulators (2014).

Table 2.2 above presents some examples of sanctions that can be imposed by the water regulator or the competent authority (as in the case of Malaysia). Box 2.4 describes specific examples from selected countries.

Box 2.4. Application of monetary penalties, examples from selected countries

In Albania, the regulator applies monetary sanctions to the utilities when they function without licence or when they fail to respect license conditions with fines from LEK 5 000 (EUR 350) up to LEK 300 000 (EUR 2 000). Failures to apply the Regulatory Authority decisions on tariffs or to pay financial obligations to the regulatory authority within deadlines are also subject to fines up to LEK 100 000 (EUR 700).

In Australia/New South Wales, if the private utilities do not provide adequate information requested by the regulator to undertake its review, the regulator can impose a fine up to AUD 500 000 (EUR 336 000) for the first day on which each contravention occurs, and AUD 20 000 (EUR 13 000) for each subsequent day (not exceeding 25 days).

In Bulgaria, the water regulator can impose fines to the utilities but also to the responsible members in the management body for the following regulatory infringements:

- If the utilities fail to present the next business plan, the regulator can impose a fine of EUR 10 000 to EUR 25 000 to the utility and an additional fine of EUR 1 000 to 2 500 for the responsible official/member of the management body;
- The delivery of WWS services at prices higher than those approved by the regulator is subject to monetary penalties from EUR 100 000 to 250 000 along with an additional fine for the responsible official/member of the management body; and
- The failure to present information requested by the regulator is subject to a fine of EUR 15 000 up to EUR 50 000.

The repetition of the above cases of breaches leads to a fine, which is up to three times higher than the original ones. The member of the management body will be also deprived from the right to keep their respective position from one to two years.

In Belgium/Flanders, the water regulator can impose administrative fines in case of failure or incorrect delivery of requested data/information. For the first offense, and after two written warnings a monetary penalty of maximum 0.01% of the total revenues (excl. VAT) for integral water services (drinking water and waste water) will be imposed. For each subsequent violation within the same calendar year, the percentage will be doubled.

Source: OECD Survey on the Governance of Water Regulators (2014).

Customer engagement and protection

Twenty five regulators report a function related to customer engagement and 25 have a role in customer protection. Overall, only 5 regulators do not have any role in any of these two areas. In the case of UK/England and Wales, a specific body (the Consumer Council for Water)[3] has been established to address both dimensions. However, even though "OFWAT does not generally deal with individual consumer complaints or enquiries", it has articulated a procedure for consumer complaints on its website.[4] OFWAT is also committed to water and wastewater companies developing a customer engagement framework in relation to price setting.[5]

Customer engagement through consultation with a view to ensure regulatory quality is the subject of a specific section below on tools and mechanisms to ensure regulatory quality. In relation to customer protection, 26 regulators report having articulated a procedure for consumers to follow when making complaints. In the vast majority of cases, customers are required to claim their rights first directly to the water operators. Then if no satisfactory answer is received, the customer can turn to the regulator or a specific body (Box 2.5). Overall, according to the survey answers, customers can claim their right to the regulator in 21 cases. Other authorities who have a role in customer dispute resolution involve various government agencies, customers' associations, ombudsman (10 regulators report the existence of an ombudsman) and courts. In Portugal, operators maintain complaints book, where customers can write their complaints, which is then analysed by the regulator.

Box 2.5. Consumer complaint procedure in selected territories

In UK/England and Wales, OFWAT has articulated a procedure for consumer complaints on its website around three components: *i)* Contacting the company; *ii)* In case the customer is not satisfied with the company's response; and *iii)* The recourse to the Consumer Council for Water to investigate, www.ofwat.gov.uk/consumerissues/complaints/.

In Kosovo, the first appeal body is the service provider. Then the customers can claim their rights to the Consumer Consultative Committee (CCC), a regional body which organises monthly meetings, with the service operators on price reviews and performances. Customers can also resort to Courts.

In UK/Scotland, the Water Industry Commission directs household customers first to the company's formal complaints procedure, and in case they are not satisfied, to the Scottish Public Services Ombudsman (SPSO), www.watercommission.co.uk/view_Complaints.aspx.

In US/Maine, the Public Utilities Commission first directs the consumers to the utility to attempt to resolve the complaint. If the utility is unable to do so, consumers are invited to contact the Commission's Consumer Assistance Division (CAD) itself, www.maine.gov/mpuc/consumer/file_complaint.shtml.

In Uruguay, URSEA first directs the consumers to the utility. In case the utility does not answer or does not provide a satisfactory answer within 15 days, the claim can be made to the regulator, www.ursea.gub.uy/Inicio/Usuarios/Reclamos. The situation is similar in Peru, with the difference that the utility has 30 days to solve a complaint. (www.sunass.gob.pe/websunass/index.php/usuarios/2013-06-26-23-35-09)

Source: OECD Survey on Applying Better Regulation in the Water Service Sector (2014) and websites of regulators.

The number of complaints handled by regulators annually varies widely, but overall reflects the fact that the regulator is not the first dispute resolution instance (Table 2.3).

Table 2.3. **Complaints handled by the regulator, selected regulators**

	Albania	Armenia	Bulgaria	Chile	UK/England & Wales	Kosovo	Malaysia	Mozambique	Peru	Portugal	Uruguay
Complaints handled annually by the regulator	180	222	625	12 000	4 500	120	800	300	22 000	4 500	60
Share in overall number of complaints in the water sector (in %)	0.88	0.05	5.69	2.07	2.98	0.60	0.05	6	8.63	13.64	0.19

Source: OECD Survey on the Governance of Water Regulators (2014).

Figure 2.12. **Dispute resolution mechanisms between the authorities and the operators**

(Number of regulators/34)

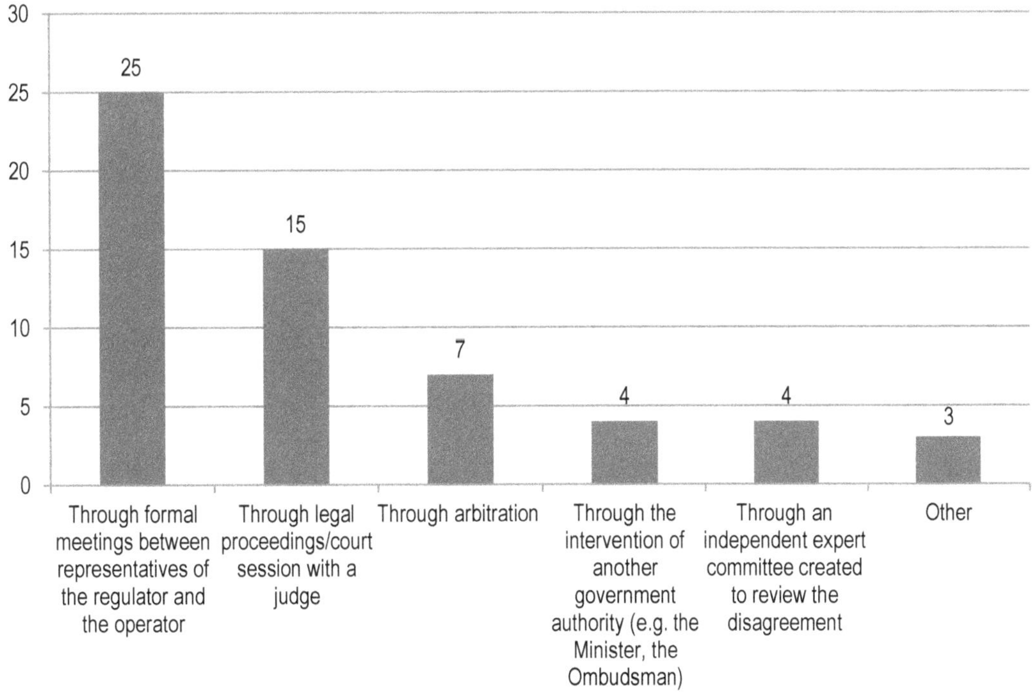

Mechanism	Number
Through formal meetings between representatives of the regulator and the operator	25
Through legal proceedings/court session with a judge	15
Through arbitration	7
Through the intervention of another government authority (e.g. the Minister, the Ombudsman)	4
Through an independent expert committee created to review the disagreement	4
Other	3

Source: OECD Survey on the Governance of Water Regulators (2014).

Regulators also play a role as a mediator between line ministries and water operators (Figure 2.12). In case of disputes between the responsible authorities – be they line ministries or the regulator itself –, the first mediation instance is provided through formal meetings between the regulator and the operator (in 24 cases).

Internal organisation

The OECD *Best Practice Principles for the Good Governance of Regulators* highlights that regulatory decisions and functions should be conducted with upmost integrity to ensure that there is confidence in the regulatory regime. This is critical for ensuring that the rule of law is maintained, for encouraging investment and having an enabling environment for inclusive growth. To support its activities, the regulator needs a governance structure that combines its human, financial and organizational resources in an effective way. An important aspect of this structure is the leadership of the regulatory agency, in the form of a governance board, Commission or a single director/CEO, and the decision making process by which regulatory decisions are taken. Agency staff play a crucial role as they bring a level of expertise and professionalism that determines the quality of the regulator's work. The rules for appointments, recruitment and termination and the professional competencies gathered across regulatory agencies all play an important role to determine the capacity of the regulator. Answers to the survey shed light on the different approaches to mobilising financial resources, staffing and managing the internal organisation of the regulator. They highlighted the wide variety of situations across regulators.

Personnel

Size of regulatory bodies

The direct comparison of staff across regulators is not an easy task given that the information is not fully comparable. For instance, some of the numbers provided by the regulators include the board or commission members, while others do not. In some cases the staff of the regulatory body includes inspectors, which inflates considerably the staff members of the regulatory body: in Chile, 90 of the 201 employees are inspectors; in Portugal, 21 of the 77 staff take care of audits and inspections. The multi-sector regulators make it particularly difficult to evaluate the number of staff dedicated to water given that a number of services (generally support services) are joint. In the case of Hawai, there is no specific staff dedicated to the regulation of water sector. The staff – comprised of legal, engineers, audit and research – works on all utility sectors. In Italy, 12 staff are directly allocated to water regulation, but the inspection activities are shared with electricity and gas. In Latvia, 8 staff work on water regulation in the municipal services department, but the Commission counts overall 118 staff, including in 4 support departments (economic analysis, legal support, accounting and administrative units), which are shared across sectors, and 5 commissioners making decisions on all regulated sectors.

To avoid some of the difficulty, Figure 2.13 clusters regulators in 4 groups according to staff numbers. The information as received from regulators on their size is provided in the regulators factsheet at the end of the report. Figure 2.13 shows that there is a variety of sizes across regulatory bodies. The water staff of multi-sector regulators is consistently smaller than the staff of water specific bodies: among the 10 bodies with less than 10 employees, 9 are multi-sector bodies, while the 4 biggest bodies are water specific entities.

Other factors may explain the differences, including the characteristics of the water industry, the size of the population served and the range of functions carried out by the regulator and its powers. It is expected that regulators with significant enforcement powers and a depth of expertise would translate in a sizeable staff. Some activities of the regulator may also be particularly staff intensive. As mentioned above the regulators that have inspection functions in relation to quality standards will maintain an important body of inspectors that will translate into a substantially bigger size (Chile). Regulators with a responsibility for building capacity of smaller operators, such as ERSAR in Portugal, will also need human resources to visit the various operators and work directly with them. By contrast, VMM, the water regulator in Belgium/ Flanders, is a regulatory body that is dedicated to drinking water only and it has mainly an advisory role in many of the functions that it performs. The regulator in Indonesia regulates the Jakarta area only. In both cases, these features may explain the smaller size of the regulator.

Figure 2.13. **Number of employees**

(Number of regulators/34)

	Less than 10 employees	Between 11 and 29 employees	Between 30 and 100 employees	More than 100 employees
Number	10	12	8	4
Regulators	Belgium/Flanders, Australia /ACT*, Australia/Victoria*, Estonia*, UK/N. Ireland*, US/Maine*, US/Ohio*, US/Pennsylvania*, US/Tennessee*, Uruguay*	Albania, Armenia*, Australia/NSW*, Australia/WA *, Brazil/RS*, Bulgaria*, Ireland*, Italy*, Indonesia, Kosovo, Latvia*, UK/Scotland	Colombia, Hungary*, Mozambique, Portugal*, Romania*, Ukraine*, US/Hawaii*, US/West Virginia*	Chile, Malaysia, Peru, UK/E&W

Note: * Multi-sector regulators.

Source: OECD Survey on the Governance of Water Regulators (2014).

The expertise embedded in the regulatory body

The excellence of the technical staff is ensured for all regulators through a competitive recruitment process. In addition, in more than half the cases (18), the agency is exempt from the usual civil servant salary rules, which allows paying competitive wages. This is likely to attract a greater pool of applicants from both public and private sectors, thereby increasing experience and expertise.

The survey constitutes a first attempt at collecting systematic data on the job families and expertise embedded in regulatory bodies. Figure 2.14 illustrates the variety of situations across a selection of water regulators. The water technical expertise constitutes an important share of the expertise in most regulators – as illustrated by the prominence of the "engineering" category in most countries. The importance of economic and legal expertise is also consistent across regulators. However, their respective share varies widely across territories. This may reflect real differences in competences, or different understanding of the categories proposed in the survey. A substantial number of regulators reacted to the survey question and identified other relevant categories that did not appear in the initial question. OFWAT for instance commented that some 40% of OFWAT staff did not fit with the job categories proposed in the survey. In this specific case, missing families include procurement, facilities management, finance, business support, IT, human resource, programme management, and casework.

Figure 2.14. **Job families and professions represented in selected regulatory agencies**

(In percentage)

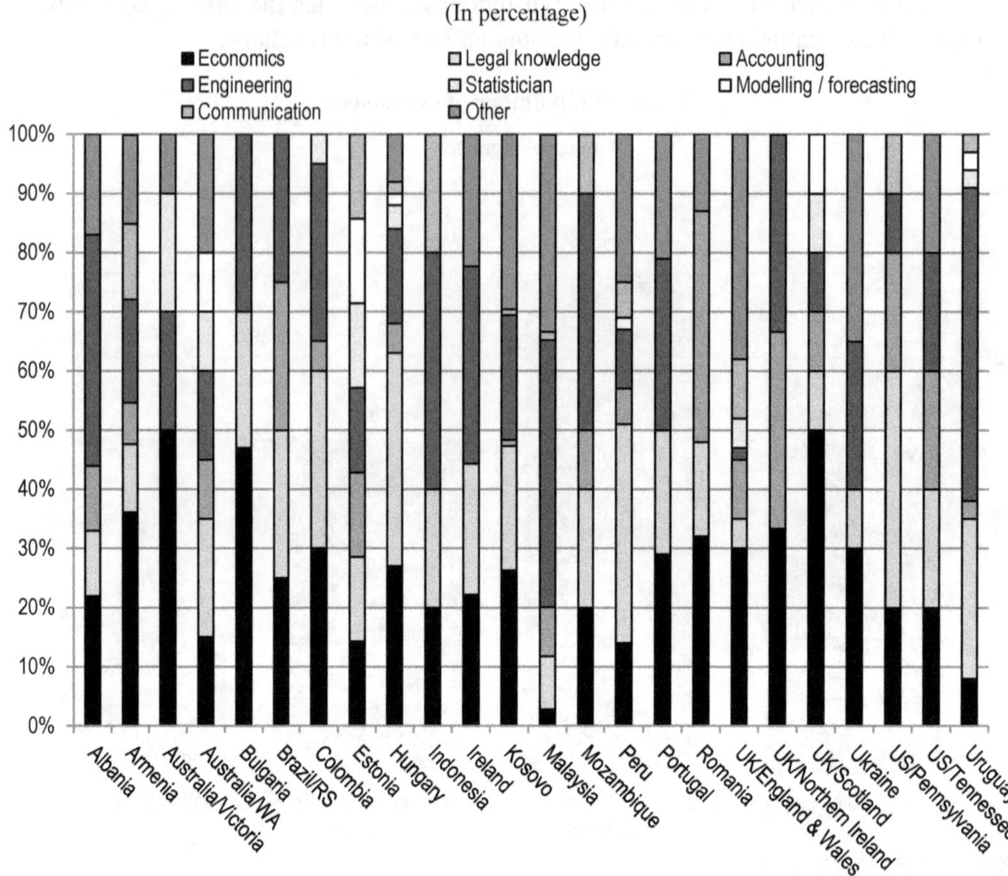

Source: OECD Survey on the Governance of Water Regulators (2014).

Terms of office

The *OECD Best Practice Principles for Regulatory Policy: The Governance of Regulators* identifies the importance of the terms of appointment of the CEO and board members. Whilst long term or renewed appointments provide a certain amount of certainty and institutional grounding, and may prevent some political interference by drawing a clear line between the regulator and electoral or political cycles, the Principles state that "There should also be a limit to the terms of appointment of the CEO and board members to allow for renewal of the leadership and prevent long appointments".

In two cases, terms of office of the head of the regulatory body are not limited in their duration: Belgium/Flanders and Romania. In these two cases, the regulator is a ministerial department or a part of a governmental agency and the rules of employment are those that apply more generally to civil servants. In all other cases, responses to the survey show that terms of office of the agency heads and board members are limited in time – with a duration that varies between 2 years (Malaysia) and 7 years (Hungary and Italy), with most regulators enjoying a term of 5 or 6 years (Figure 2.15). However, when the possibility of renewing the term is taken into account, unlimited or unspecified term renewal allows the cumulated duration of appointment to be indefinite in 17 cases (Figure 2.16). Whether this has led in practice to long stay in office of the agency heads and board members was not captured by the survey.

Figure 2.15. **Duration of the term of office of the agency head or board members**

(Number of regulators/34)

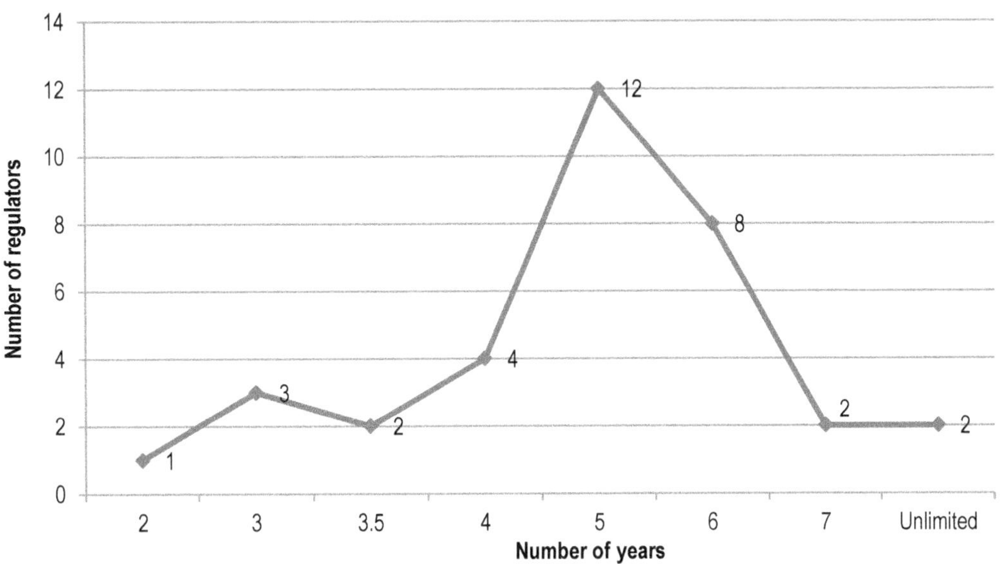

Note: Duration of the term of office was averaged for Australia/WA, Australia/NSW and Scotland based on the ranges provided.

Source: OECD Survey on the Governance of Water Regulators (2014).

Figure 2.16. **Cumulated length of the terms of office of the agency head or board members**

(Number of regulators/34)

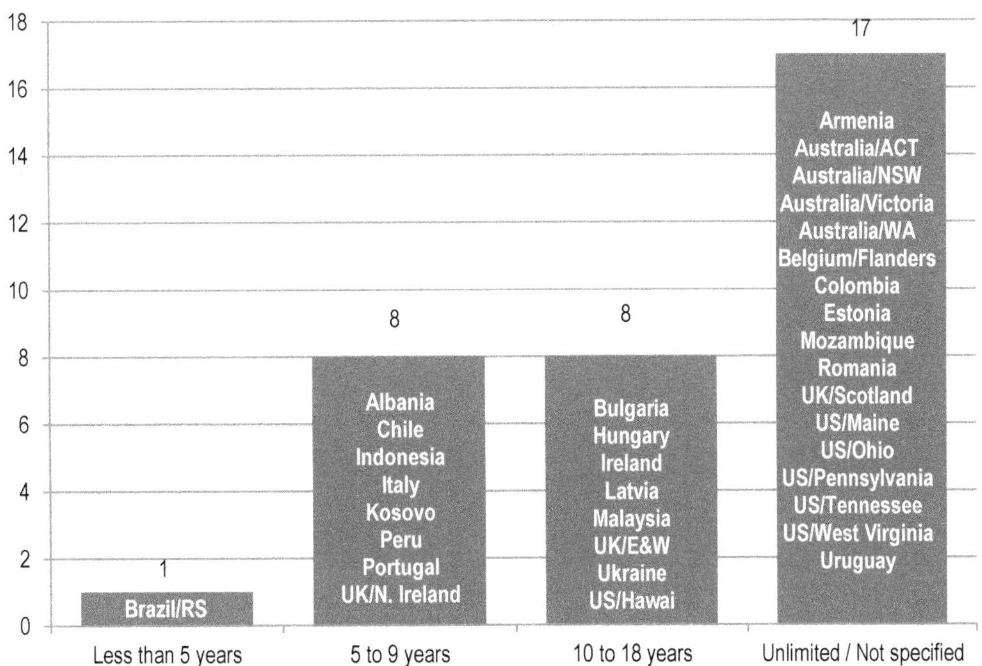

Source: OECD Survey on the Governance of Water Regulators (2014).

For the majority of regulators (in 27 cases), the criteria for appointing members of a regulator's governing body, and the grounds and process for terminating their appointments are explicitly stated in legislation. In Bulgaria, for instance, the law provides for the minimum education level and work experience of the Commission members. Other dimensions of the employment of the head/board members are also closely regulated. For instance, while the agency head/board members are allowed to take jobs in the private water sector after their term in office, there is usually a cooling period before they are allowed to do so in particular if it is to join one of the utilities that they used to regulate. The cooling period may extend from 6 months to 2 years. The agency head/board members can be dismissed from office through a government decision in 18 cases. In 7 cases, it is done through a parliamentary decision. In other cases, the president or the prime minister may be involved.

Financial resources

Operating budget of regulators

The average annual operating budget varies widely across regulators (Figure 2.17). In some multi-sector regulator cases, the budget was provided for the whole of the agency and not only for the water part (they are indicated by "*" in Figure 2.17), making it difficult to compare across regulators. Regulators with the biggest staff size (Chile and UK/England and Wales) have more substantial budgets.

Figure 2.17. **Regulator's average annual operating budget**

(in EUR and in number of regulators/32)

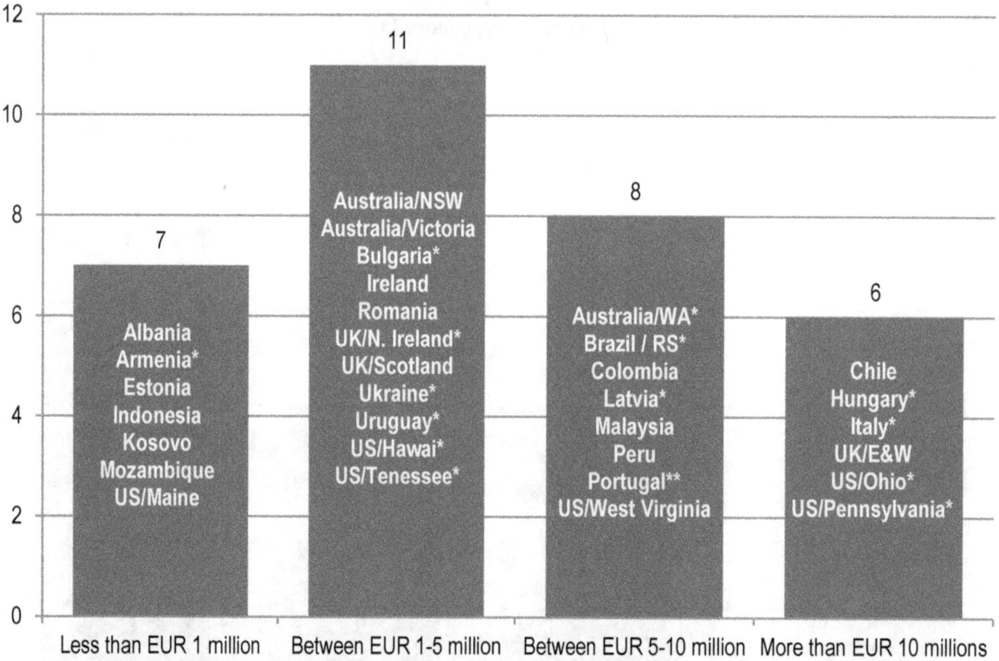

Notes: Excluding Australia/Australian Capital Territory and Belgium/Flanders.

* Multi-sector regulators which provided their total budget (no breakdown for water activities).

** Data for Portugal cover both water and waste activities.

Source: OECD Survey on the Governance of Water Regulators (2014).

When the information was available, the share of the regulator's operating budget was measured in percentage of the average turnover of the regulated industry, as shown in Table 2.4. In the cases of multi-sector regulators, it is important to note that the information was not always available for the water sector separately from the other sectors, which explains the higher percentage. Shares of regulators' annual operational budget to the annual turnover of the regulated industry vary substantially.

Table 2.4. **Share of the regulator's average annual operating budget to the total turnover of the regulated industry**

(In percentage)

Countries	Share (%)
Albania	0.73
Australia/New South Wales	0.15
Australia/Victoria	0.07
Bulgaria*	0.7
Brazil/RS*	0.17
Chile	1.17
Estonia	0.17
Hungary*	1.9
Kosovo	1.44
Latvia*	5.77
Malaysia	0.71
Mozambique	2.00
Peru	1.00
Portugal**	0.38
UK/England & Wales	0.18
UK/Northern Ireland*	0.38
UK/Scotland	0.19
Ukraine*	0.40
US/Maine	0.38
US/Tennessee*	1.71
Uruguay*	0.08

Notes: * Multi-sector regulators which provided their total budget (no breakdown for water activities).

** Data for Portugal cover both water and solid waste activities.

Source: OECD Survey on the Governance of Water Regulators (2014).

Sources of funding

Based on the answers to the questionnaire, the main sources of revenue for the regulator's activities are fees from service providers (in 24 cases) and budget funding (in 14 cases) (Figure 2.18). In 4 cases, regulators also report monies from penalties and fines (Hungary, Italy, Portugal and US/West Virginia), and interest earned on investments and trust funds (Australia/Capital Territory and New South Wales, Ireland and Malaysia) as sources of revenue. IPART in Australia/New South Wales is also able to charge fees to agencies for services in specific projects with the Premier's approval.

While the budget of a regulator determines its capacity to carry out its functions, its sources of funding provide a measure of the regulator's autonomy in decision making. For three quarters of regulators, more than 70% of their budget comes from services to the regulated industry through levies or fees for instance (Figure 2.18). In 7 cases, government funding contributes to more than 70% of the regulator's budget. In 6 cases, government budget is the only source of funding for the regulator (Belgium/Flanders, Bulgaria, Chile, Estonia, Romania and Ukraine). It is noteworthy that in some cases, the regulator collects revenue from regulated entities, but transfers it to the state budget before being allocated an allowance to cover its expenditures. This is for example the case in Bulgaria, where the regulator receives a monthly allowance from the state budget – which is approximately half the revenues collected by SEWRC, the regulator.

Twenty six regulators over 34 report having separate annual budget allocations, with autonomy in the implementation of the allocated budget. However, these regulators do not fully correspond to the 26 regulators who reported being financed through services to the regulated industry. In the cases of Australia/New South Wales, Belgium/Flanders, Estonia and Romania, despite the totality or most of its budget coming from government funding, the regulator enjoys autonomy in the allocated budget. Conversely, in the cases of Albania, Armenia, Indonesia, Peru and Uruguay, where more than 70% of the regulator's budget come from fees to the regulated industry, the regulator does neither have separate annual budget allocations nor autonomy in the implementation of the allocated budget. In three cases (Bulgaria, Chile and Ukraine), the regulator has neither a separate source of funding, nor autonomy of budget use. Overall, two-thirds of the regulators enjoy separate budget allocations and a source of financing which is independent from the government.

Figure 2.18. **Regulator's financing sources**

(Number of regulators/34)

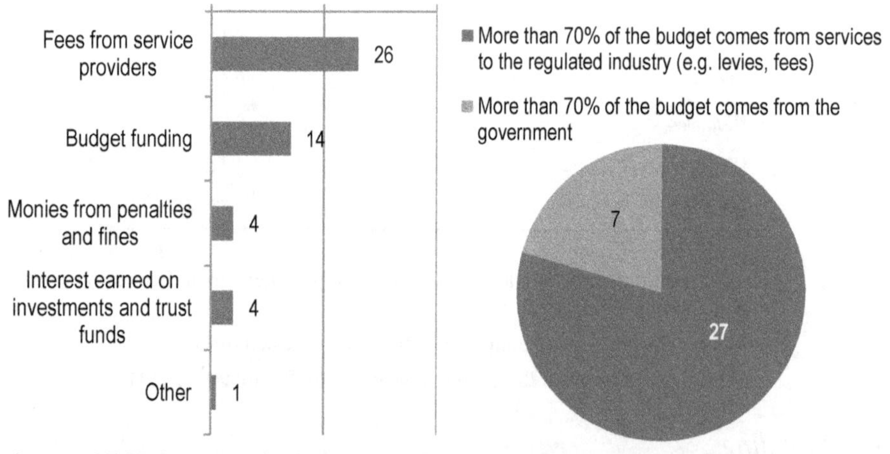

Source: OECD Survey on the Governance of Water Regulators (2014).

When the regulator is funded by fees from service providers, the fee structure varies across territories (Figure 2.19). The level of fees is usually a function of regulatory costs. It is borne by the industry depending on its turnover, or on its revenue (over the past year or over as an average over several years), or as a percentage of tariff. Other considerations may play a role, such as the number of customers, property value (US/West Virginia) or the industry structure (in Indonesia, the regulator is financed equally across the two water companies it regulates).

Figure 2.19. **Fee structure**

(Number of regulators/26)

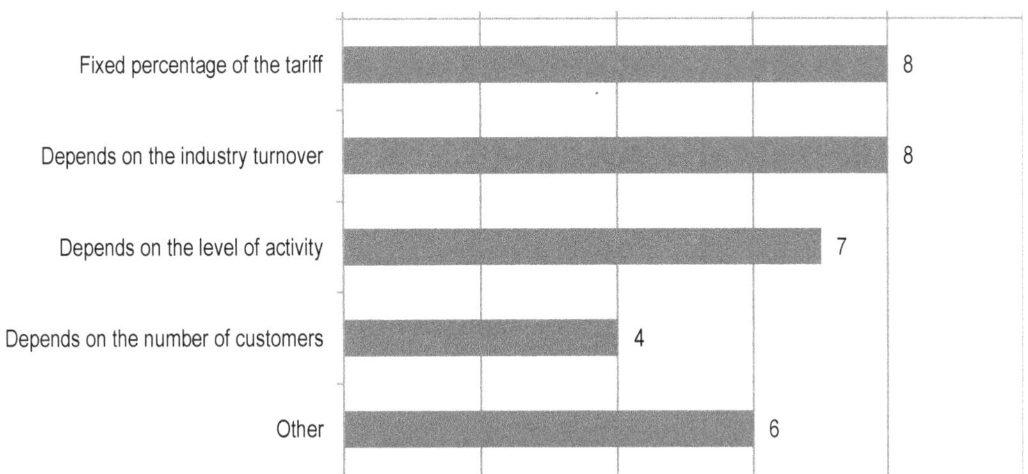

Notes: The question was not applicable to regulators mainly funded from government budget (Australia/New South Wales, Belgium/Flanders, Bulgaria, Chile, Estonia, Romania and Ukraine). Information from Australia/Victoria is missing.

Source: OECD Survey on the Governance of Water Regulators (2014).

Accountability mechanisms

Accountability and transparency of regulators is the subject of Chapter 4 of the OECD *Best Practice Principles for Regulatory Policy: The Governance of Regulators*. The Principles identify three groups of stakeholders to which regulators are generally accountable to: ministers and the legislature; regulated entities; and the public. A regulator is usually tasked with protecting consumers' interests and receives delegations and powers from the government to act on this objective. An important aspect of this relates to the mechanisms available to regulators to monitor and disseminate information about the level and quality of services provided by the operators. Subjecting the activities of the regulator to scrutiny is important to enhance the integrity of the regulatory process and ultimately to secure the trust and respect of all constituents.

Countries have a number of mechanisms to ensure that water regulators are held accountable. The regulator may be required to report regularly and publicly to the legislature on its objectives and activities or/and be submitted to periodical evaluation to ensure that it is meeting its responsibilities with integrity, honesty and objectivity. Accountability can be safeguarded through transparency requirements on regulatory decisions and the possibility of revision and appeal. In particular, the *OECD Best Practice Principles for Regulatory Policy: The Governance of Regulators* highlights the following:

- Regulators should report to ministers or legislative oversight committees on all major measures and decisions on a regular basis and as requested;

- Key operational policies and other guidance material, covering matters such as compliance, enforcement and decision review, should be publicly available; and
- Regulated entities should have the right of appeal of decisions that have a significant impact on them, preferably through a judicial process.
- This chapter takes stock of the variety of accountability mechanisms in place across the range of water regulators who answered the survey.

Formal accountability

Based on the survey answers, 32 regulators are accountable by law to the government or to the parliament (22 to the government and 16 to parliament). In two exceptions, Ireland and US/Tennessee, regulators report that their actions may be challenged by courts. In six cases (Albania, Belgium/Flanders, Italy, Portugal, UK/Northern Ireland and Uruguay), regulators have both accountability vis-à-vis the government and the parliament. In one case, there is a stated accountability vis-a-vis the regulated entities (Portugal). In several cases, regulators report being accountable by law to the public via their annual report or other communication means such as on their website.

Reporting requirements on the regulator's activities

Twenty nine regulators are required to report to the legislature on their performance. Where there is such a requirement, it is done on an annual basis in 24 cases. In Italy, Peru and Portugal, it is done at the request of parliament. In the case of Portugal, this has lately led to a frequency of reporting of twice a year. In the cases of Bulgaria and Uruguay, the situation dictates the need for reporting. This reporting requirement may be for information only in some countries (Ireland).

All regulators, excluding two (Estonia and Peru), face a legislative requirement to produce an annual report on their activities. In the case of Peru, the regulator voluntarily publishes one. All regulators report making the information publically available on their website. However, in a number of cases, the reports are not easily accessible – they do not appear clearly on the website.

Thirty regulators face a legal requirement to publish information related to various dimensions of the regulator's activity. Information for publication concerns mainly: the costs of operating the regulator (in 22 cases), the decisions, resolutions and agreements reached by the regulator (in 21 cases), and the governance structure of the regulator (in 19 cases) (Figure 2.20). In 5 cases, the regulator faces legislative requirements to publish all of this information (4 in the US: Maine, Ohio, Pennsylvania, Tennessee and Romania). In 4 other cases (Australia/Victoria, Brazil/Rio Grande Do Sul, Kosovo and Scotland), the regulator faces all disclosure requirements, except for fines and minutes of public consultation. There is not such a legal requirement in Belgium/Flanders, Estonia, Ireland and Malaysia, although it has been a common voluntary practice by regulators to report on these elements in their annual report.

Figure 2.20. **Legislative requirements in place requiring the publication of the following information**

(Number of regulators/30)

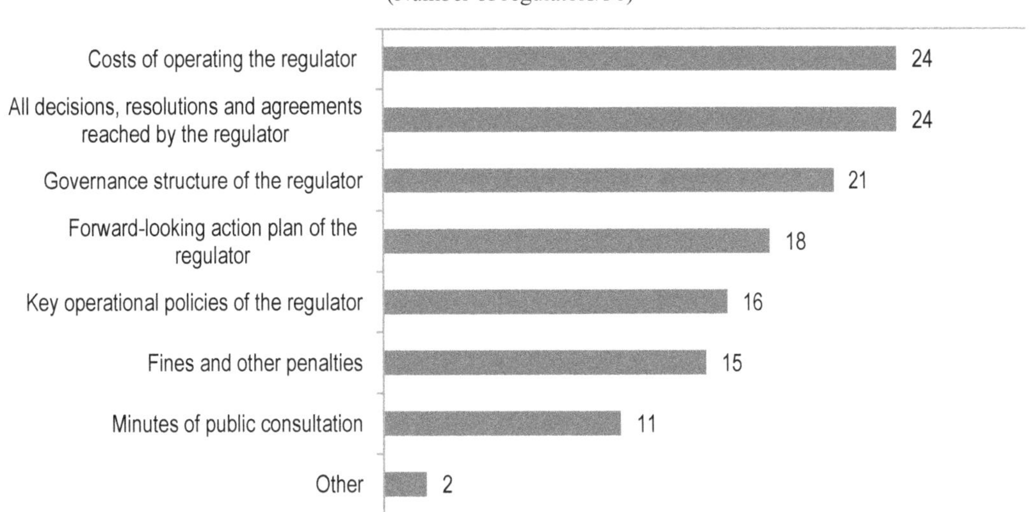

Note: Excluding Belgium/Flanders, Estonia, Ireland and Malaysia.

Source: OECD Survey on the Governance of Water Regulators (2014).

Appeal processes

All respondents but one report one or several procedures to appeal against decisions taken by the regulator. In two cases, however, the only recourse is through the regulator itself. In most cases (30), this is taken to the courts directly. In five cases, there is a possibility of appeal through the competition authority (Chile, UK/England and Wales, Malaysia, UK/Scotland and UK/Northern Ireland). In 5 instances, specific commissions or panels deal with the complaints against the decisions by the regulator – it is for example the case in the state of Victoria or in Kosovo. In a number of countries, several mechanisms are simultaneously in place – typically in Chile and Malaysia. Table 2.5 provides examples of decisions that can be appealed and the grounds for appeals.

Table 2.5. **Examples of decisions that can be appealed and the grounds for appeals**

Country	Decision
Albania, Armenia, Estonia, Indonesia, Italy, Kosovo, Latvia, Ukraine, US/Tennessee and West Virginia, Uruguay	All decisions of regulator can be appealed in Court without restriction.
Bulgaria, Chile, Mozambique, Portugal	Binding decisions on the ground that they breach the law.
Australia/Capital Territory	Decisions to grant or refuse a licence is appealable on administrative grounds. Price Direction. Grounds are not specified.
Australia/Victoria	A person that is aggrieved by a requirement, disclosure or determination can appeal on the following grounds (Essential Services Commission Act 2001): The requirement was not made in accordance with the law; or is unreasonable having regard to all the relevant circumstances.

Table 2.5. **Examples of decisions that can be appealed and the grounds for appeals** (*cont.*)

	- The decision was not made in accordance with the law; or is unreasonable having regard to all the relevant circumstances. - There has been bias; or the determination is based wholly or partly on an error of fact in a material respect.
Colombia	In particular decisions, providers may submit appeals if they disagree with the decision.
Ireland	All decisions on grounds of reasonableness – judicial review will assess whether CER made reasonable rather than right decision.
Scotland	Final Determinations, on grounds of inaccuracy of information and breach of regulator's mandate.
US/Hawaii and Maine	When Decisions made are beyond jurisdiction, arbitrary, not in the public interest, unconstitutional.

Source: OECD Survey on the Governance of Water Regulators (2014).

Tools and mechanisms to ensure regulatory quality

Regulators have a range of tools at their disposal to ensure the quality of the regulatory processes. In particular, the Recommendation of the Council on Regulatory Policy and Governance adopted in 2012 by OECD members highlights that "regulatory agencies should be required to follow regulatory policy including engaging with stakeholders and undertaking regulatory impact assessment when developing draft laws or guidelines and other forms of soft laws".[6] This section focuses on the extent to which regulatory policy tools have been mainstreamed in the activities of regulators.

Figure 2.21. **Uptake of regulatory instruments**

(Number of regulators/34)

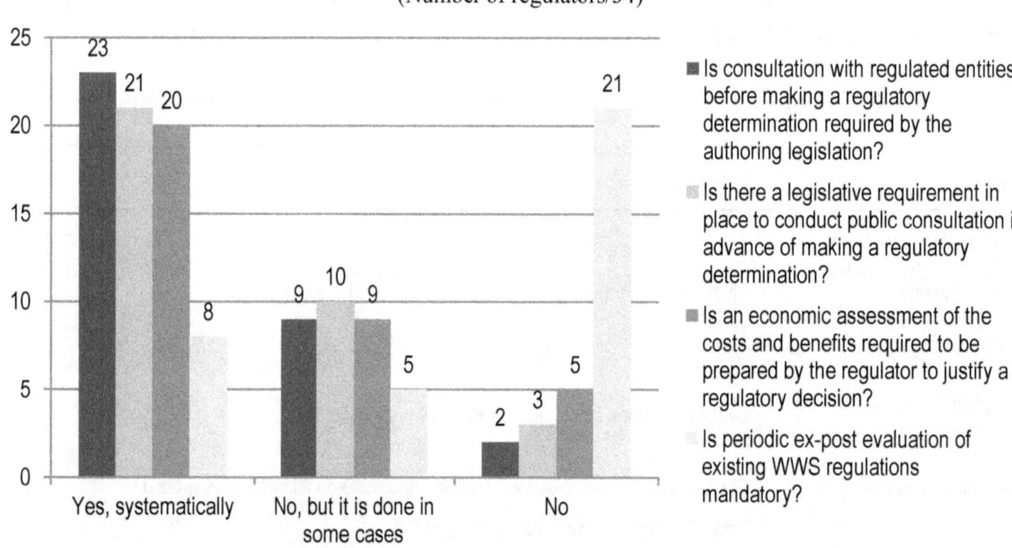

Source: OECD Survey on the Governance of Water Regulators (2014).

Results from the survey support the view that water regulators routinely resort to consultation and cost/benefit analysis to ensure the quality of the regulatory process (Figure 2.21). By contrast, systematic *ex post* evaluation of regulatory decisions remains the exception.

Consultation with operators and consumers

Among the tools available to regulators, consultation with regulated entities, and more generally with the public at large, is largely used (Figure 2.21). Based on the answers to the survey, 22 regulators have a consultation strategy.[7] There is a legislative requirement to consult with regulated entities before making a regulatory determination for 23 regulators. There is also a legislative requirement to conduct public consultation in advance of making a regulatory decision for 21 regulators. When not required by law, water regulators carry out consultation on a voluntary basis. Only in 2 cases regulated entities are not consulted (Hawaii and US/West Virginia), and in 3 cases public consultation is not carried out (Chile, Estonia and Hungary).

Consultation with regulated entities

Areas for consultation with regulated entities include mostly tariff setting (27 regulators), quality and technical standards (respectively 19 and 17 regulators) (Figure 2.22). Regulators also report routinely involving regulated entities in the discussion of licensing rules, the development of normative acts or of industry codes and guidelines, the conditions and performance assessment of service provision, and the business plans and related operating and capital expenditure of regulated companies. Disclosure of the results of consultation with regulated entities is an important tool to protect the regulator against the risk of capture. Of the 32 regulators who engage with regulated entities, 17 report making the results of the consultation publicly available in a systematic manner, 8 make it available sometimes and 7 do not make it available at all.

Figure 2.22. **Areas subject to consultation with regulated entities**

(Number of regulators/31)

Area	Number of regulators
Tariff setting	27
Quality standards	19
Technical standards	17
Licensing	12
Other	10

Note: Excluding Belgium/Flanders, US/Hawaii and US/West Virginia.

Source: OECD Survey on the Governance of Water Regulators (2014).

Public consultation

Public consultation is widely carried out by regulators, through a range of different means (Figure 2.23) and on a wide variety of topics (Figure 2.24). Targeted consultation is the norm. Regulators, for instance, carry out informal consultation with selected groups

(27 regulators) or circulate regulatory proposals to selected experts for comments (17 regulators). Twenty four regulators consult with regulators from other sectors. These mechanisms co-exist with broader consultation initiatives via public meetings open to any citizen (for 25 regulators) or via broad calls for public comments on regulatory intentions (for 22 regulators). More specific mechanisms are also used. In UK/Scotland, for instance, the establishment of a "Customer Forum" seeks to identify and understand customers' priorities to secure the most appropriate outcome for customers, through adequate price and service levels. The economic regulator of Scottish Water has the task of ensuring that Scottish Water is adequately funded and a statutory duty to promote the interests of customers by setting prices for water and wastewater services at the lowest reasonable overall cost. The Customer Forum's role is to determine what, in the customers' interest, should be considered reasonable.[8]

Figure 2.23. **Forms of public consultation routinely used by the regulator**

(Number of regulators/31)

Informal consultation with selected groups	27
Public meetings open to any citizen	25
Consultation with other sector regulators	24
Public notice of regulatory intentions and a broad call for comments from the general public	22
Circulation of regulatory proposals/decisions to selected experts for comment	17
Preparatory public commission/committee	8
Other	2

Note: Excluding Chile, Estonia and Hungary.

Source: OECD Survey on the Governance of Water Regulators (2014).

However, feedback of public consultation is not systematically disclosed: 7 of the 31 regulators who carry out public consultation do not make the views of the participants public. In most cases, uncertainty remains regarding the way public feedback is taken into account by regulators. Box 2.6 provides selected examples of how the views expressed in the consultation process are taken into account. Overall, little is known about the performance of the consultation process. Twenty two regulators over 31 report that they have no process to monitor the quality of consultation. Among the exceptions, IPART in New South Wales conducts a stakeholder survey every 2-3 years, which includes the quality of the consultation processes.

Figure 2.24. **Issues for public consultation**

(Number of regulators/31)

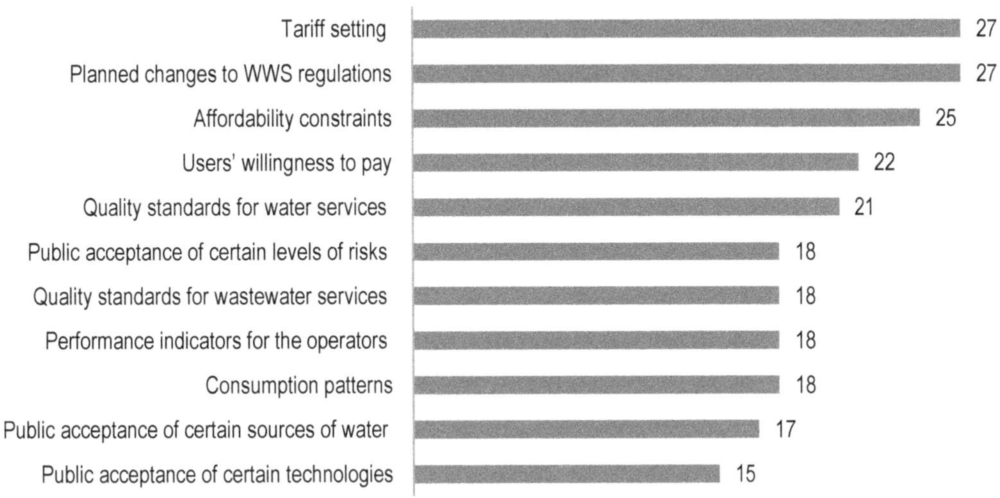

Note: Excluding Chile, Estonia and Hungary.

Source: OECD Survey on the Governance of Water Regulators (2014).

Box 2.6. **Taking into account the views expressed in the consultation process, selected examples**

In general, the regulator collects the opinions expressed by the consumers and the operators and reviews them, with a view to take into consideration the views that are deemed justified and potentially amend the regulatory proposals ("to reach the optimal rule" as mentioned in Italy):

- IPART in Australia/New South Wales collates all the views of stakeholders received during the review process and presents these to the Tribunal for consideration.
- In Bulgaria, the Commission examines and summarises all opinions received during the Open Meetings and Public Hearings, and accepts them or not. Motives for the decision are published on the Commission's website.
- In Colombia, changes may result from the consultation process, but whatever the use of the comments received, related decision must be motivated.
- In US/Tennessee, if the views are sufficient in number, they are tallied, and considered in the process with substantially equal weight as those of staff and any other parties.
- In other US States, the collected views are expressly addressed in written Commission orders (Maine) or recorded as part of the docket record (Hawaii).

Source: OECD Survey on the Governance of Water Regulators (2014).

Impact analysis of regulatory decisions

According to the survey, cost/benefit analysis is routinely used by the vast majority of water regulators to justify regulatory decisions (Figure 2.21). Twenty regulators report being required to systematically prepare an economic assessment of the costs and benefits to justify a regulatory decision (e.g. on tariff settings, terms and conditions of market access, service standards). Nine regulators do it in some cases, in particular for six of them in relation to tariff determinations. Five regulators report not doing it at all (Colombia, Ireland, Romania, US/Maine and US/West Virginia).

The survey also included a question related to whether the regulator routinely analyses the impact of new WWS regulation/rules when the regulator has a rule making power. The aim of this question was to differentiate between the regulatory decision made by the regulator as part of its regulatory activities as defined by the law and its activity related to the development or changes in norms and regulations in the sector. However, responses to the question show that for most regulators, this distinction was not clear.

In the majority of cases, it is possible to infer from the answers that the regulator either does not have a role in developing new regulations in the sector; or is not the responsible oversight authority to carry out regulatory impact assessment (it is clearly stated in the cases of Australia/Victoria and Belgium/Flanders). In other cases, impact analysis of new regulations – through Regulatory Impact Analysis (RIA) or other tools – is not a commonly used tool. Portugal, for instance, reports that while ERSAR does not implement a formal RIA procedure, it carries out some sort of impact analysis and is currently considering adopting a more formal RIA procedure. Overall, it can be estimated that it is likely a third of the sample of regulators who carry some forms of impact assessment of new norms and regulations adopted in the water sector. A concrete example of use by a regulator of impact assessments is provided by OFWAT in UK/England and Wales (Box 2.7).

Box 2.7. **OFWAT's policy on impact assessments**

According to its policy on impact assessments published in April 2011, OFWAT will normally include impact assessments when consulting on major changes to its policies. This excludes cases where OFWAT is:

- carrying out formal enforcement action (for which specific procedures are laid down in law);
- using its formal powers to resolve complaints or disputes;
- implementing legislation (which will have been approved by Parliament and subject to impact assessment by the sponsoring government department) except where OFWAT has significant discretion about how it implements the statutory requirement;
- publishing proposals which draw together a range of options which have been subject to separate consultation or impact assessment; or
- proposing a policy that already includes a form of impact assessment, such as its reviews of price limits.

The impact assessment will include the following:

- the purpose of the action OFWAT proposes to take;
- why OFWAT proposes to take action in a particular area ('what is the problem?');
- the intended impact of the action ('what does OFWAT want to achieve?');

Box 2.7. OFWAT's policy on impact assessments (*cont.*)

- the options under consideration ('what alternative actions could be taken?');
- the preferred option ('what action OFWAT is proposing to take?').

In addition, the impact assessment will contain detailed evidence of the action under consideration. OFWAT will compare the likely impact of our proposed action against the impact of taking no action (the "do nothing" option). A typical impact assessment might include the following evidence:

- the costs and benefits to consumers, particularly the contribution different options would make to delivering on consumer objective;
- the costs and benefits to those OFWAT regulates;
- the effect on competition;
- the costs and benefits to the environment, considering particularly the water environment;
- the contribution towards meeting requirements set out in the 'ministerial guidance';
- the contribution towards long-term sustainable development;
- the contribution towards innovation.

An example is OFWAT's impact assessment of implementing accounting separation for water companies.

Source: www.ofwat.gov.uk/aboutofwat/pap_pos_2011impact.pdf; www.ofwat.gov.uk/competition/pap_tec_091218_accsep_ia.pdf.

Ex post evaluation of regulations and regulatory decisions remain the exception. It is done only by a handful of countries mostly in Eastern Europe. Malaysia and Ukraine provide two different illustrations of this approach. In Malaysia, SPAN has recently started using RIA approach in setting regulations, as well as *ex post* evaluation, as part of an overall country reform aimed at implementing good regulatory practices. This is carried out through targeted feedback on regulatory impacts through consultation and review process. A quick-scan method is used to determine problems which need to be resolved. In Ukraine, the regulator carries out periodic controls of the efficiency of the regulatory act through qualitative and quantitative comparison of current and previous regulatory act efficiency index.

Burden reduction

Based on the answers to the survey, 14 regulators have completed a measurement of administrative burdens (i.e. the costs imposed on regulated entities when complying with obligations stemming from WWS regulations). However, again, interpretation of the question varied widely across regulators. A number of regulators associated this measurement with the evaluation of impacts on utilities of price and other determinations. In some territories (Malaysia, US/Ohio, US/Pennsylvania), however, measurement of administrative burdens is done with each proposed law and rule. Other regulators report having recently completed a measurement of administrative burdens (in 2013 for

Australia/New South Wales, Hungary, UK/England and Wales, and US/Maine). Some regulators have undertaken such measurement as part of a transition to a new approach to regulation. This is for instance the case in Australia/New South Wales, where the regulator has undertaken such a measurement in 2013 as part of its regulation review based on which the regulator has adopted a management system approach to regulation. In the US/Maine, the regulator reports that the reform of regulations is being evaluated for the purpose, among other things, of reducing administrative burdens.

A wide range of administrative simplification measures are used (Figure 2.25). The most widely used include: putting time limits on regulatory decision making (in 25 cases); streamlining reporting requirements for operators (23 cases); streamlining of existing regulations (23 cases); guidance to operators on how to comply with regulations (22 cases); plain language drafting (20 cases); offering e-government services (18 cases); and assigning a person to handle queries (17 cases).

Figure 2.25. **Administrative simplification measures used in relation to WWS regulations**

(Number of regulators/33)

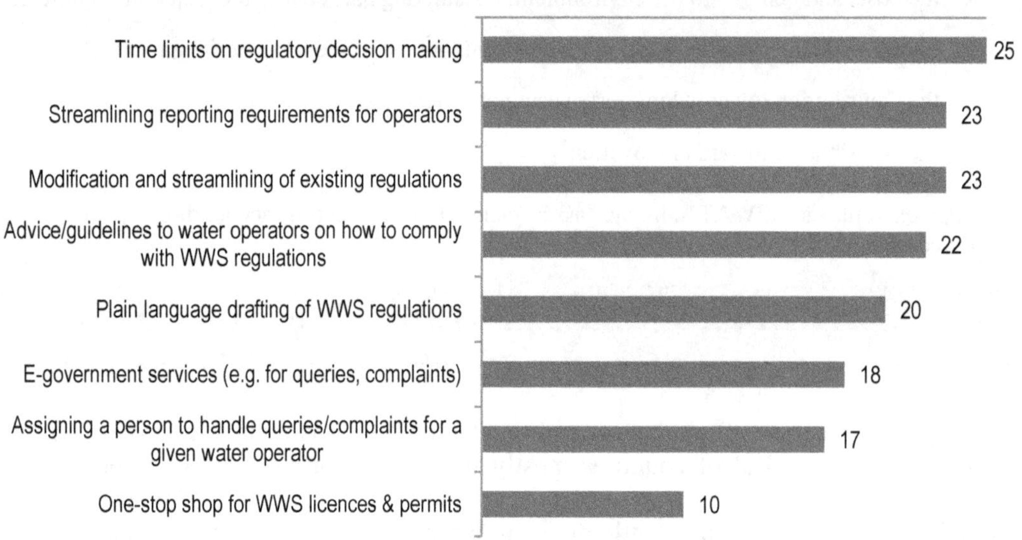

Note: Excluding Ireland where no such measure has been implemented for water regulation yet.

Source: OECD Survey on the Governance of Water Regulators (2014).

Notes

1. www.gov.uk/government/uploads/system/uploads/attachment_data/file/221043/pb13884-sps-seg-ofwat-201303.pdf.

2. www.watercommission.co.uk/UserFiles/Documents/WICS%20Performance%202012-13.pdf.

3. The Consumer Council for Water (www.ccwater.org.uk): "The Consumer Council for Water (CCWater) represents water and sewerage consumers in England and Wales. (…) Our job is to make sure that the collective voice of consumers is heard in national water debate and that consumers remain at the heart of the water industry. We will also take up consumers' complaints if they have tried and failed to resolve issues with their water companies. We aim to settle 70% of complaints within 20 working days and settle 85% within 40 working days."

4. www.ofwat.gov.uk/consumerissues/complaints/.

5. www.ofwat.gov.uk/future/monopolies/fpl/customer.

6. www.oecd.org/gov/regulatory-policy/2012-recommendation.htm.

7. As an example, the Charter of Consultation for Australia/Victoria can be found at: www.esc.vic.gov.au/getattachment/1bb604dc-bb77-4220-9b1c-63ec0ae89b71/Charter-of-Consultation.pdf.
   For Uruguay: www.ursea.gub.uy/Inicio/Usuarios/.

8. http://customerforum.org.uk/about-us/.

Bibliography

Karnitis, E. and A. Virtmanis (2011), "Multi-sectoral regulation of services of general economic interest: Ten-year experience of Latvia", Public Utilities Commission of Latvia, Riga, www.sprk.gov.lv/uploads/doc/Multiregulator.pdf.

OECD (2014), *OECD Best Practice Principles for Regulatory Policy: The Governance of Regulators*, OECD Publishing, Paris, http://dx.doi.org/10.1787/9789264209015-en.

OECD (2012), "Recommendation of the Council on Regulatory Policy and Governance", www.oecd.org/gov/regulatory-policy/2012-recommendation.htm.

Chapter 3

Water regulators factsheets

This chapter provides a one-page profile for all water regulators involved in the OECD Survey. This profile offers key facts that characterise the water sector under the jurisdiction of the regulator to define the scope of its activity. It includes key facts on the water regulator itself based on information collected through the OECD Survey. It also provides a synthetic map of institutions involved in the regulation of the water services to contextualise the activity of the regulator and acknowledge the wide variety of institutional arrangements.

ALBANIA

Key facts of the water sector

Territory

- Surface (km²): 28 748
- Population size (million): 2.774 (World Bank, 2013)
- Population density (inhabitants/km²): 96 (World Bank, 2013)
- Share of urban population: 52% of total population (CIA, 2010)
- Number of households (million): 0.571 (General Directorate of Water Supply and Sewerage, 2013)
- Average household size: 4.52 persons (estimate based on the population served by the utility divided by the number of water connections) (Water Regulatory Authority, 2014)

Data on the sector activity

- Number of water operators: 58 (OECD Survey, 2014)
- Water main networks (km pipelines): 7 478 (transmission and distribution systems, Water Regulatory Authority, 2014)
- Number of active connections (million): 0.631 (Water Regulatory Authority, 2014)
- Abstracted water volume (million m³): 272 (Water Regulatory Authority, 2014)
- Average consumption (litre/resident/day): 74 (Water Regulatory Authority, 2014)
- Non-Revenue Water (%): 68 (IBNET, 2012)
- Turnover of the water industry (EUR): 43 million (OECD Survey, 2014)

Key facts of the water regulator

- Year of establishment: 1996
- Water-specific regulator (incl. sanitation)
- Share of water operators covered: 100%
- Budget (EUR): 315 000
- Number of employees: 21 (incl. 5 Commissioners)

For more information:
Water Regulatory Authority of Albania
Blv. Gjergj Fishta, Nr.10
Tirana, Albania
www.erru.al
Contact: public@erru.al

Source: OECD Survey, 2014.

Institutional arrangements for water regulation

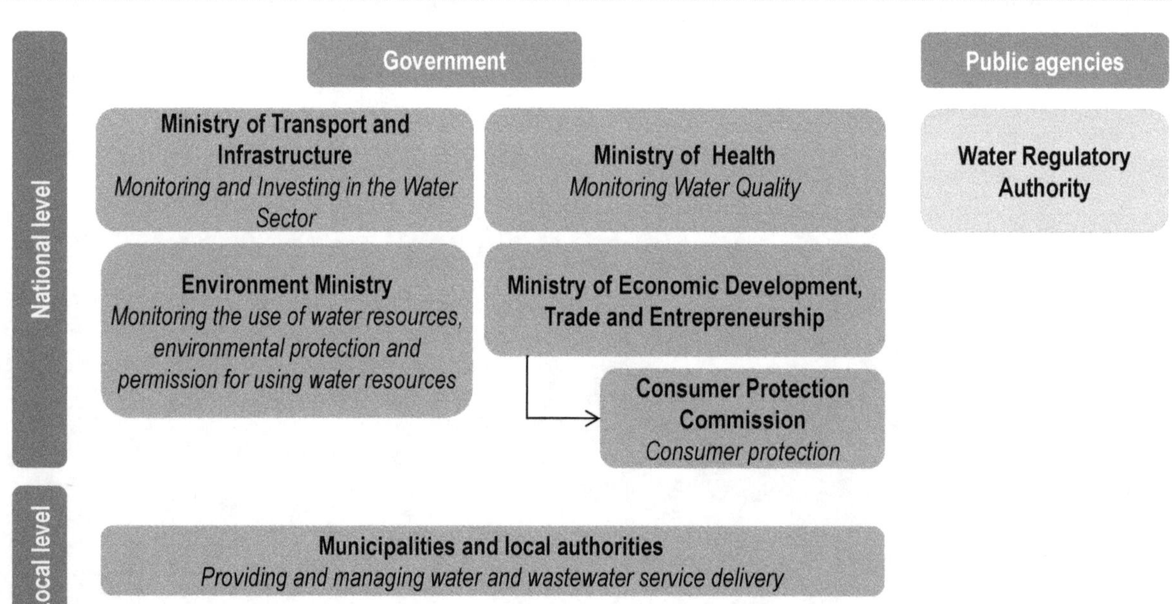

Source: OECD Survey on the Governance of Water Regulators, 2014, Water Regulatory Authority of Albania: www.erru.al and written contribution received on 8 July 2014; IBNET: www.ib-net.org; World Bank: www.data.worldbank.org/country/albania; Central Intelligence Agency: https://www.cia.gov/library/publications/the-world-factbook/index.html.

ARMENIA

Key facts of the water sector

Territory

- Surface (km²): 29 743
- Population size (million): 2.977 (WB, 2013)
- Population density (inhabitants/km²): 100 (WB, 2013)
- Share of urban population: 64.1% of total population (CIA, 2011)
- Number of households (million): 0.764 (National Bureau of Statistics, 2011)
- Average household size: 3.6 persons (Armenia Demographic and Health Survey, 2010)

Data on the sector activity

- Number of water operators: 5 (OECD Survey, 2014)
- Water main networks (km pipelines): NA
- Number of active connections (million): NA
- Abstracted water volume (million m³): 588 (Marques, 2010)
- Average consumption (litre/resident/day): 84 (Marques, 2010)
- Non-Revenue Water (in %): 83 (IBNET, 2010)
- Turnover of the water industry (EUR): 16.6 million (Marques, 2010)

Key facts of the water regulator

- Year of establishment: 2003
- Multi-sector regulator: Energy, Telecommunications, Water, Postal services and Railways
- Share of water operators covered: 100%
- Budget: AMD 523.68 million in 2013 (EUR 944 000) (total)
- Number of employees: 13 (water regulation)

Source: OECD Survey, 2014.

For more information:
Public Services Regulatory Commission of the Republic of Armenia (PSRC)
22 Saryan St,
Yerevan, Armenia 375002
www.psrc.am/en/
Contact: psrc@psrc.am

Institutional arrangements for water regulation

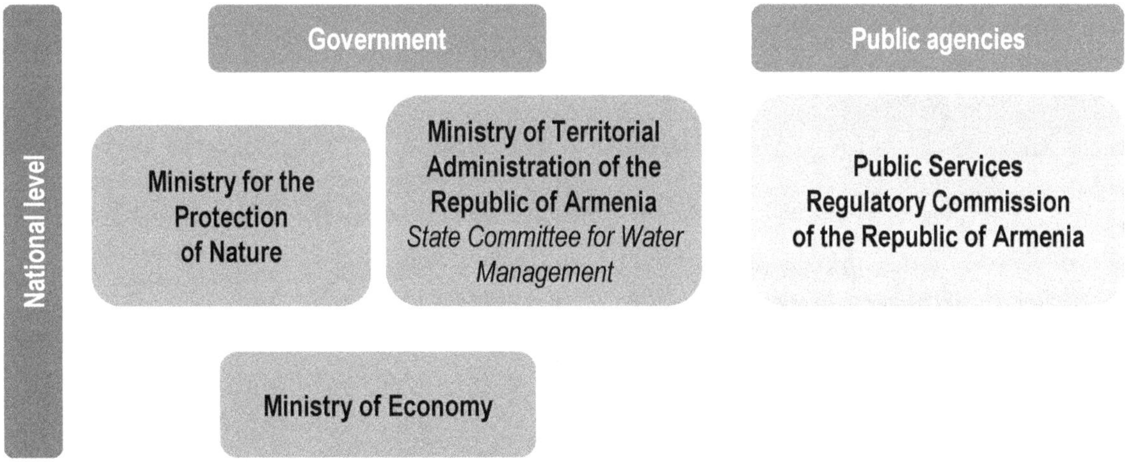

National level

Government

- Ministry for the Protection of Nature
- Ministry of Territorial Administration of the Republic of Armenia — *State Committee for Water Management*
- Ministry of Economy

Public agencies

- Public Services Regulatory Commission of the Republic of Armenia

Source: OECD Survey on the Governance of Water Regulators, 2014; Armenia Demographic and Health Survey (2010): www.dhsprogram.com/pubs/pdf/SR190/SR190.pdf; National Statistical Service of the Republic of Armenia: www.armstat.am/en/?nid=517; IBNET: www.ib-net.org and Marques, R. (2010), *Regulation of Water and Wastewater Services – An International Comparison*, IWA Publishing, London.

AUSTRALIA/CAPITAL TERRITORY

Key facts of the water sector

Territory

- Surface (km²): 2 358
- Population size (million): 0.383 (ABS, 2013)
- Population density (inhabitants/km²): 162 (ABS, 2013)
- Share of urban population: 100% of total population
- Number of households (million): 0.145 (private dwellings, ABS, 2011)
- Average household size: 2.6 persons (ABS, 2011)

Data on the sector activity

- Number of water operators: 1
- Water main networks (km pipelines): 3 219
- Number of active connections (million): 0.16
- Abstracted water volume (million m³): 46
- Average consumption (litre/resident/day): 190 (in 2011-12 – ABS, 2013)
- Non-Revenue Water (in %): NA
- Turnover of the water industry (EUR): 175 million (in 2011-12 – ABS, 2013)

Key facts of the water regulator

- Year of establishment: 1997
- Multi-sector regulator: Electricity, gas, water and sewerage
- Share of water operators covered: 100%
- Budget: N.A.
- Number of employees: 4 (water regulation)

Source: OECD Survey, 2014.

For more information:
Independent Competition and Regulatory Commission (ICRC)
Level 8, 221 London Circuit,
Canberra City ACT 2600
www.icrc.act.gov.au/
Contact: icrc@act.gov.au

Institutional arrangements for water regulation

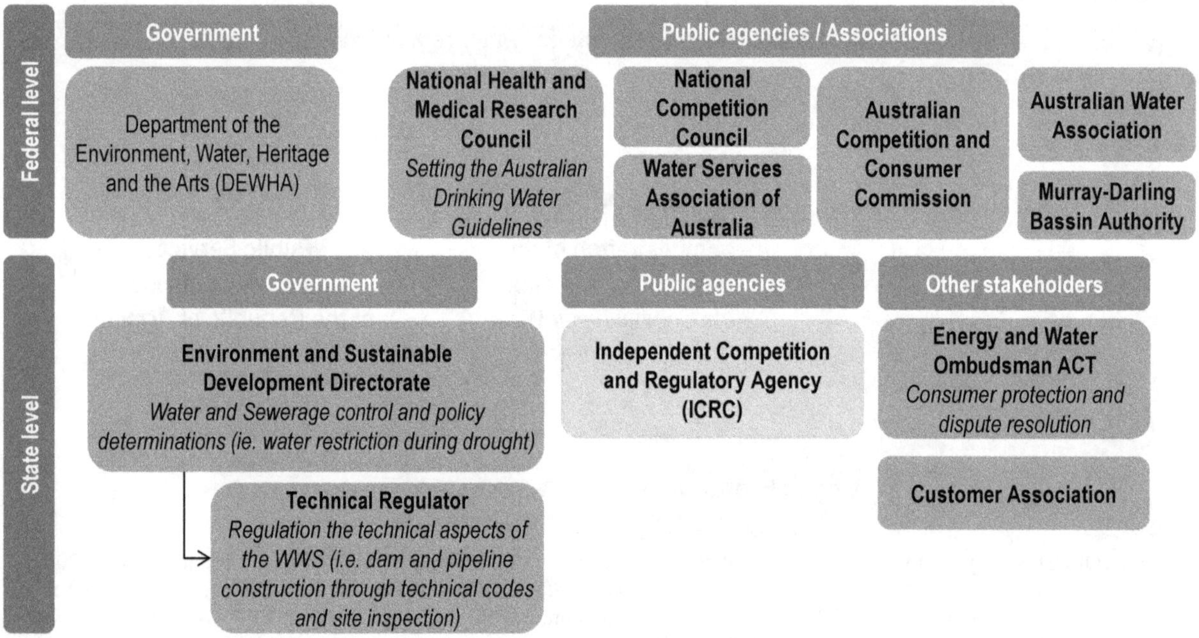

Federal level

Government

Department of the Environment, Water, Heritage and the Arts (DEWHA)

Public agencies / Associations

National Health and Medical Research Council
Setting the Australian Drinking Water Guidelines

National Competition Council

Water Services Association of Australia

Australian Competition and Consumer Commission

Australian Water Association

Murray-Darling Bassin Authority

State level

Government

Environment and Sustainable Development Directorate
Water and Sewerage control and policy determinations (ie. water restriction during drought)

Technical Regulator
Regulation the technical aspects of the WWS (i.e. dam and pipeline construction through technical codes and site inspection)

Public agencies

Independent Competition and Regulatory Agency (ICRC)

Other stakeholders

Energy and Water Ombudsman ACT
Consumer protection and dispute resolution

Customer Association

Sources: OECD Survey on the Governance of Water Regulators, 2014, Australian Bureau of Statistics: www.abs.gov.au/ausstats/abs@.nsf/mf/3101.0; ABS 2011 Census: www.censusdata.abs.gov.au/census_services/getproduct/census/2011/quickstat/8?opendocument&navpos=95 and www.abs.gov.au/ausstats/abs@.nsf/lookup/4610.0main+features302011-12#australiancapitalterritory.

AUSTRALIA/NEW SOUTH WALES

Key facts of the water sector

Territory

- Surface (km²): 800 809 (ABS, 2014)
- Population size (million): 7 501 (ABS, 2014)
- Population density (inhabitants/km²): 9.3 (ABS, 2014)
- Share of urban population: 86% (ABS, 2014)
- Number of households (million): 2.865 (private dwellings, ABS, 2011)
- Average household size: 2.6 persons (ABS, 2011)

Data on the sector activity

- Number of water operators: 123
- Water main networks (km pipelines): 29 718 (for the 20 regulated utilities only, IPART 2014)
- Number of active connections (million): 2.227 (for the 20 regulated utilities only, IPART 2014)
- Abstracted water volume (million m³): 7 490 (combining drinking water, recycled water and rural raw water for the 20 regulated utilities only, IPART 2014)
- Average consumption (litre/resident/day): 192 (in 2011-12 – ABS, 2013)
- Non-Revenue Water (in %): 7% (for the 20 regulated utilities only, IPART 2014)
- Turnover of the regulated water industry (EUR): 2 369 million (OECD Survey, 2014)

Key facts of the water regulator

- Year of establishment: 1993
- Multi-sector regulator: Energy, Transport, Water
- Share of water operators covered: 16% (20 operators)
- Budget: 5.127 million AUD in 2013 (water regulation) (3.5 million EUR)
- Number of employees: 24 (water regulation, excl. legal and support functions)

Source: OECD Survey, 2014.

For more information:
Independent Pricing and Regulatory Tribunal (IPART)
Level 15
2-24 Rawson Place
Sydney NSW 2000
www.ipart.nsw.gov.au/Home
Contact: ipart@ipart.nsw.gov.au

Institutional arrangements for water regulation

Sources: OECD Survey on the Governance of Water Regulators, 2014; IPART; Australian Bureau of Statistics (ABS): www.abs.gov.au.

AUSTRALIA/VICTORIA

Key facts of the water sector

Territory

- Surface (km²): 237 000
- Population size (million): 5.8 (ABS, 2013)
- Population density (inhabitants/km²): 24.3 (ABS, 2013)
- Share of urban population: NA
- Number of households (million): 2.278 (private dwellings, ABS, 2011)
- Average household size: 2.6 persons (ABS, 2011)

Data on the sector activity

- Number of water operators: 19 (OECD Survey, 2014)
- Water main networks (km pipelines): 45 632 km
- Number of active connections (million): 2.46
- Abstracted water volume (million m³): 671 (Marques, 2010)
- Average consumption (litre/resident/day): 153 (in 2011-12 – ABS, 2013)
- Non-Revenue Water (in %): 9.5% (Marques, 2010)
- Turnover of the water industry (EUR): 3 380 million (OECD Survey, 2014)

Key facts of the water regulator

- Year of establishment: 2004
- Multi-sector regulator: Energy, Water, Transport
- Share of water operators covered: 100%
- Budget (2012-13):
- Total: AUD 16.7 million (EUR 11.5 million)
- Water: AUD 3.5 million (EUR 2.4 million)
- Number of employees: 10 (water regulation)

Source: OECD Survey, 2014.

For more information:
Essential Services Commission (ESC)
Level 37/2 Lonsdale Street
Melbourne Victoria 3000
www.esc.vic.gov.au/Water
Contact: publications@esc.vic.gov.au

Institutional arrangements for water regulation

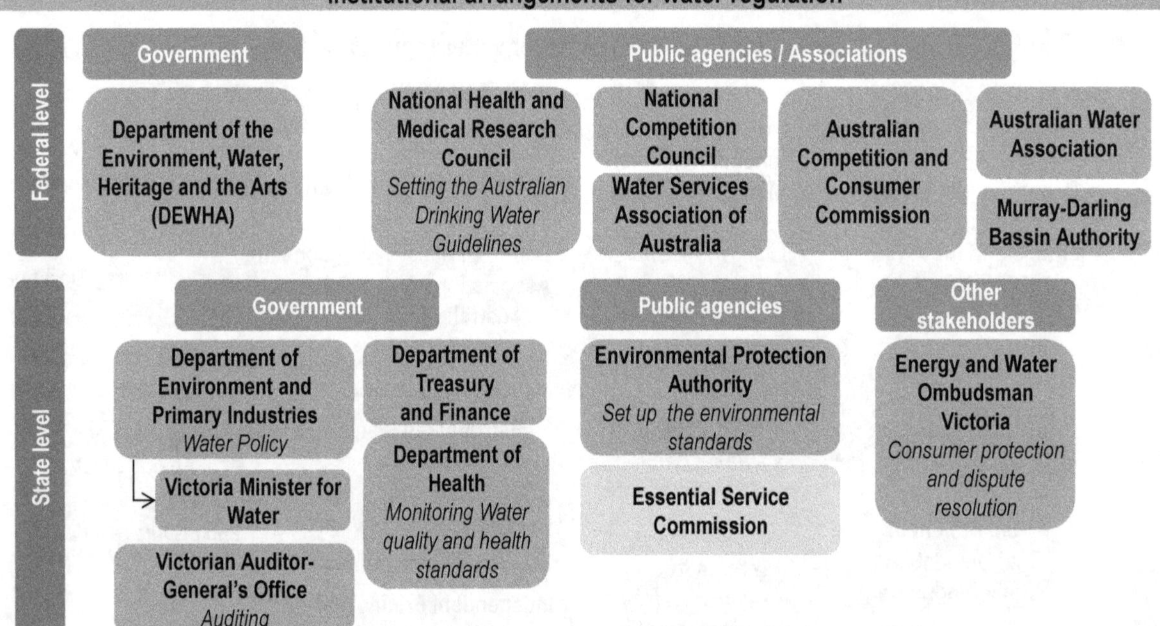

Sources: OECD Survey on the Governance of Water Regulators, 2014, Australian Bureau of Statistics: www.abs.gov.au/ausstats/abs@.nsf/mf/3101.0;
2011 Census: www.censusdata.abs.gov.au/census_services/getproduct/census/2011/quickstat/2?opendocument&navpos=95; www.abs.gov.au/AUSSTATS/abs@.nsf/Lookup/4610.0Main+Features302011-12#AustralianCapitalTerritory; and Marques, R. (2010), *Regulation of Water and Wastewater Services – An International Comparison*, IWA Publishing, London.

AUSTRALIA/WESTERN AUSTRALIA

Key facts of the water sector

Territory

- Surface (km²): 2 645 000
- Population size (million): 2.5 (ABS, 2013)
- Population density (inhabitants/km²): 0.95 (ABS, 2013)
- Share of urban population: 78.2% of total population (ABS 2012-2013)
- Number of households (million): 0.961 (number of private dwellings; ABS, 2011)
- Average people per household: 2.6 persons (ABS, 2011)

Data on the sector activity

- Number of water operators: 34 (OECD Survey, 2014)
- Water main networks (km pipelines): 34 633 km (Water Corporation Annual Report 2013 and Urban National Performance Report 2012-13)
- Number of active connections: 1 029 600 properties (Water Corporation Annual Report 2013 and Urban National Performance Report 2012-13)
- Abstracted water volume (million m³): 311 (Marques, 2010)
- Average consumption (litre/resident/day): 348 (in 2011-12 – ABS, 2013)
- Non-Revenue Water (in %): 10% (Marques, 2010)
- Turnover of the water industry: AUD 996.4 million (EUR 692 million) (Water Corporation Annual Report 2013 and Urban National Performance Report 2012-13)

Key facts of the water regulator

- Year of establishment: 2005
- Multi-sector regulator: Electricity, Gas, Rail and Water
- Share of water operators covered: 100%
- Budget: AUD10 million (EUR6.5 million)
- Number of employees: 12 (water)

Source: OECD Survey, 2014.

For more information:
Economic Regulatory Authority (ERA)
Level 4, Albert Facey House
469 Wellington Street
Perth WA 6000
www.erawa.com.au/
Contact: records@erawa.com.au

Institutional arrangements for water regulation

Federal level

Government
- Department of the Environment, Water, Heritage and the Arts (DEWHA)

Public agencies / Associations
- National Health and Medical Research Council – *Setting the Australian Drinking Water Guidelines*
- National Competition Council
- Water Services Association of Australia
- Australian Competition and Consumer Commission
- Australian Water Association
- Murray-Darling Bassin Authority

State level

Government
- Department of Environment
- Department of Water
- WA Department of Health – *Monitoring Water quality and health standards*

Public agencies
- Economic Regulatory Authority

Other stakeholders
- Energy and Water Ombudsman WA – *Consumer protection and dispute resolution*
- Customer Association

Sources: OECD Survey on the Governance of Water Regulators, 2014; Marques, R. (2010), *Regulation of Water and Wastewater Services – An International Comparison*, IWA Publishing, London; Australian Bureau of Statistics: www.abs.gov.au/ausstats/abs@.nsf/mf/3101.0 and www.abs.gov.au/ausstats/abs@.nsf/Products/3218.0~2012-13~Main+Features~New+South+Wales?OpenDocument;
2011 Census: www.censusdata.abs.gov.au/census_services/getproduct/census/2011/quickstat/5?opendocument&navpos=220 and www.abs.gov.au/AUSSTATS/abs@.nsf/Lookup/4610.0Main+Features302011-12#AustralianCapitalTerritory;
Water Corporation Annual Report 2013 and Urban National Performance Report 2012-13: (www.nwc.gov.au/publications/topic/nprs/npr-2013-urban).

BELGIUM/FLANDERS

Key facts of the water sector

Territory

- Surface (km²): 13 522
- Population size (million): 6.4 (VMM, 2013)
- Population density (inhabitants/km²): 471 (VMM, 2013)
- Share of urban population: 52% of total population, 2010 (OECD, 2012)
- Number of households (million): 2.7 (VMM, 2013)
- Average household size: 2.3 persons (VMM, 2013)

Data on the sector activity

- Number of water operators: 10, all public (OECD Survey, 2014)
- Water main networks (km pipelines): 62 000 (VMM, 2013)
- Number of active connections (million): 3 (VMM, 2013)
- Annual production of drinking water (million m³): 394/annual distribution: 414 owing to water purchase (VMM, 2013)
- Average consumption (litre/resident/day): 100 (VMM, 2013)
- Non-Revenue Water (in %): 17.5% (VMM, 2013)
- Turnover of the drinking water sector (EUR): 562 million in 2012 (VMM, 2013)

Key facts of the water regulator

- Year of establishment: 2010
- Water-specific regulator (excl. sanitation)
- Share of water operators covered: 100%
- Budget (EUR): 90 000 (in 2013)
- Number of employees: 3

For more information:
Flemish Environment Agency (VMM)
A. Van de Maelestraat 96
9320 Erembodegem
www.en.vmm.be/
Contact: info@vmm.be

Source: OECD Survey, 2014.

Institutional arrangements for water regulation

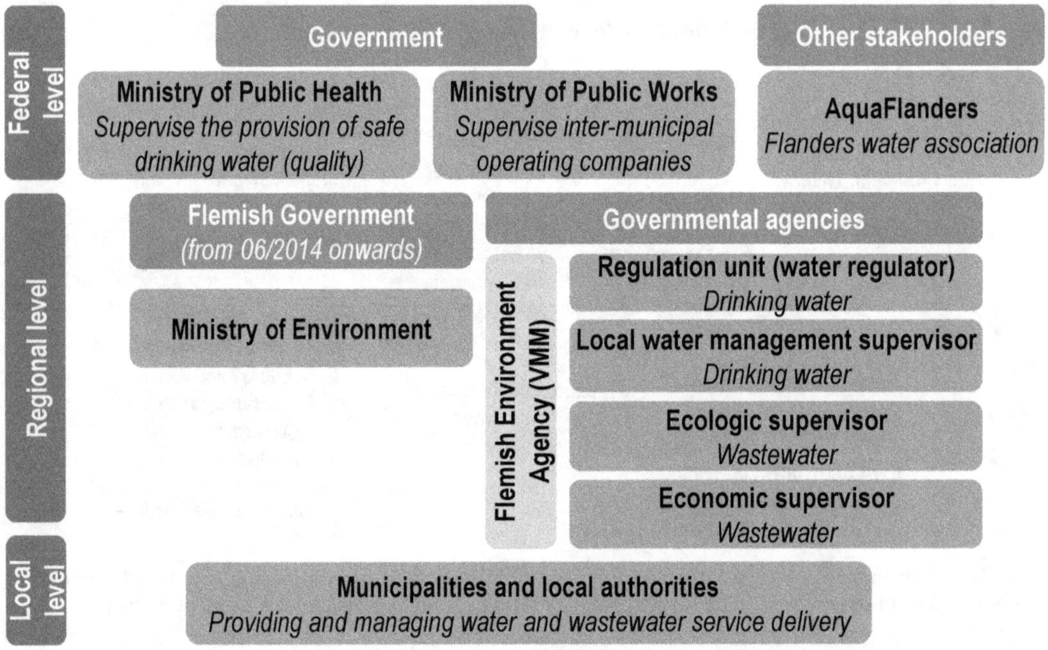

Federal level
Government
Ministry of Public Health
Supervise the provision of safe drinking water (quality)
Ministry of Public Works
Supervise inter-municipal operating companies
Other stakeholders
AquaFlanders
Flanders water association

Regional level
Flemish Government
(from 06/2014 onwards)
Ministry of Environment
Governmental agencies
Flemish Environment Agency (VMM)
Regulation unit (water regulator)
Drinking water
Local water management supervisor
Drinking water
Ecologic supervisor
Wastewater
Economic supervisor
Wastewater

Local level
Municipalities and local authorities
Providing and managing water and wastewater service delivery

Sources: OECD Survey on the Governance of Water Regulators, 2014; Flemish Environment Agency: www.en.vmm.be and written contribution received 2 May 2014; *Elaborations on the metropolitan database*, OECD (2012), *Redefining "Urban": A New Way to Measure Metropolitan Areas*, OECD Publishing, Paris, http://dx.doi.org/10.1787/9789264174108-en.

BRAZIL/RIO GRANDE DO SUL

Key facts of the water sector

Territory

- Surface (km²): 281 748
- Population size (million): 11.164 (IBGE, 2013)
- Population density (inhabitants/km²): 39.6 (IBGE, 2013)
- Share of urban population: NA
- Number of households (million): NA
- Average household size: NA

Data on the sector activity

- Number of water operators: 10 (OECD Survey, 2014)
- Water main networks (km pipelines): NA
- Number of active connections (million): NA
- Abstracted water volume (million m³): 811.6 (Marques, 2010)
- Average consumption (litre/resident/day): 170 (Marques, 2010)
- Non-Revenue Water (in %): 33.7 (Marques, 2010)
- Turnover of the water industry: BRL 12 billion (EUR 4 billion – OECD Survey, 2014)

Key facts of the water regulator

- Year of establishment: 2007
- Multi-sector regulator: Electricity, water, tolls, transports
- Share of water operators covered: 20%
- Budget: BRL 20.3 million (EUR 6.7 million)
- Number of employees: 12 (water regulation)

Source: OECD Survey, 2014.

For more information:
Agência Estadual de Regulação dos Serviços Públicos, Delegados do Rio Grande do Sul (AGERGS)
Av. Borges de Medeiros, 659 14º Andar
Porto Alegre/RS CEP 90020-023 – Brazil
www.agergs.rs.gov.br/site/index.php
Contact: not specified

Institutional arrangements for water regulation

Sources: OECD Survey on the Governance of Water Regulators, 2014; Instituto Brasileiro de Geografia e Estatística www.ibge.gov.br/home/estatistica/populacao/estimativa2013/estimativa_dou.shtm, and Marques, R. (2010), *Regulation of Water and Wastewater Services – An International Comparison*, IWA Publishing, London.

BULGARIA

Key facts of the water sector

Territory

- Surface (km²): 110 879
- Population size (million): 7.246 (Bulgarian National Statistical Institute (NSI), 2013)
- Population density (inhabitants/km²): 66.3 (Bulgarian NSI, 2011)
- Share of urban population: 73.3% (Bulgarian NSI, 2011)
- Number of households (million): not available
- Average household size: 2.4 persons (Bulgarian NSI, 2011)

Data on the sector activity

- Number of water operators: 63 (SEWRC, 2014)
- Water main networks (km pipelines): 72 103 km (SEWRC 2013)
- Number of active connections (million): 2.112 (SEWRC, 2013)
- Abstracted water volume (million m³): 1.129 (SEWRC, 2013)
- Average consumption (litre/resident/day): 203 (SEWRC, 2013)
- Non-Revenue Water (in %): 51.6 (SEWRC, 2013)
- Turnover of the water industry: BGN 535 million in 2011 (EUR 273 million – OECD Survey, 2014)

Key facts of the water regulator

- Year of establishment: 2005
- Multi-sector regulator: Electricity, natural gas, heating, water supply and sewerage services
- Share of water operators covered: 100%
- Budget: revenues EUR 4.541 million and costs EUR 1.863 million in 2011 (total)
- Number of employees:
- Water: 17 employees
- Total: 128 employees

For more information:
State Energy and Water Regulatory Commission (SEWRC)
8-10 Dondukov Blvd,1000 Sofia
www.dker.bg/indexen.php
Contact: dker@dker.bg

Source: OECD Survey, 2014.

Institutional arrangements for water regulation

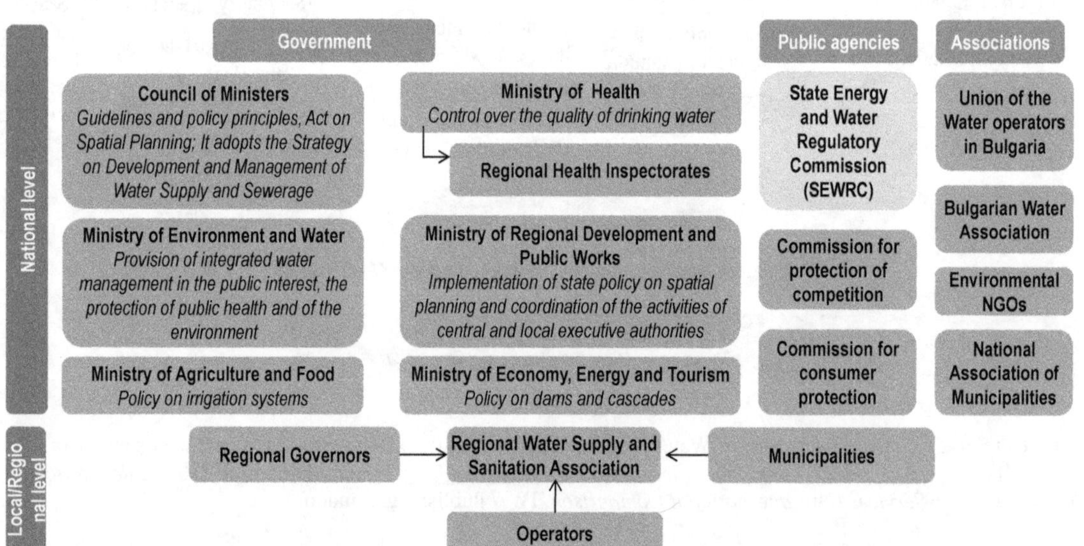

Sources: OECD Survey on the Governance of Water Regulators, 2014; SEWRC: www.dker.bg/indexen.php and written contribution received on 7 July based on Key Performance Indicators (KPIs) for 2013; OECD Family Database: www.oecd.org/els/family/oecdfamilydatabase.htm; Bulgarian National Statistical Institute (NSI): www.nsi.bg; Ministry of Regional Development and World Bank (2013), *Draft of the Strategy on development and management of WSS sector in Bulgaria*.

CHILE

Key facts of the water sector

Territory

- Surface (km²): 756 102
- Population size (million): 17.403 (OECD, 2012)
- Population density (inhabitants/km²): 23 (OECD, 2012)
- Share of urban population: 89% of total population (CIA, 2010)
- Number of households (million): 4.967 (OECD, 2011)
- Average household size: 3.7 persons (OECD, 2011)

Data on the sector activity

- Number of water operators: 58 (OECD Survey, 2014)
- Water main networks (km pipelines): 39 790 (SISS, 2014)
- Number of active connections (million): 4.8 (SISS, 2014)
- Abstracted water volume (million m³): 1 086 (SISS, 2014)
- Average consumption (litre/resident/day): 139 (SISS, 2014)
- Non-Revenue Water (in %): 34 (SISS, 2014)
- Turnover of the water industry: USD 1 539 million (SISS, 2014)

Key facts of the water regulator

- Year of establishment: 1990
- Water-specific regulator (incl. sanitation)
- Share of water operators covered: 100% (only urban population)
- Budget: USD 18 million in 2014
- Number of employees: 201, incl. 90 inspectors

For more information:
Superintendencia de Servicio Sanitarios (SISS)
Moneda 673 Piso 9
Santiago
www.siss.gob.cl
Contact: www.siss.gob.cl

Source: OECD Survey, 2014.

Institutional arrangements for water regulation

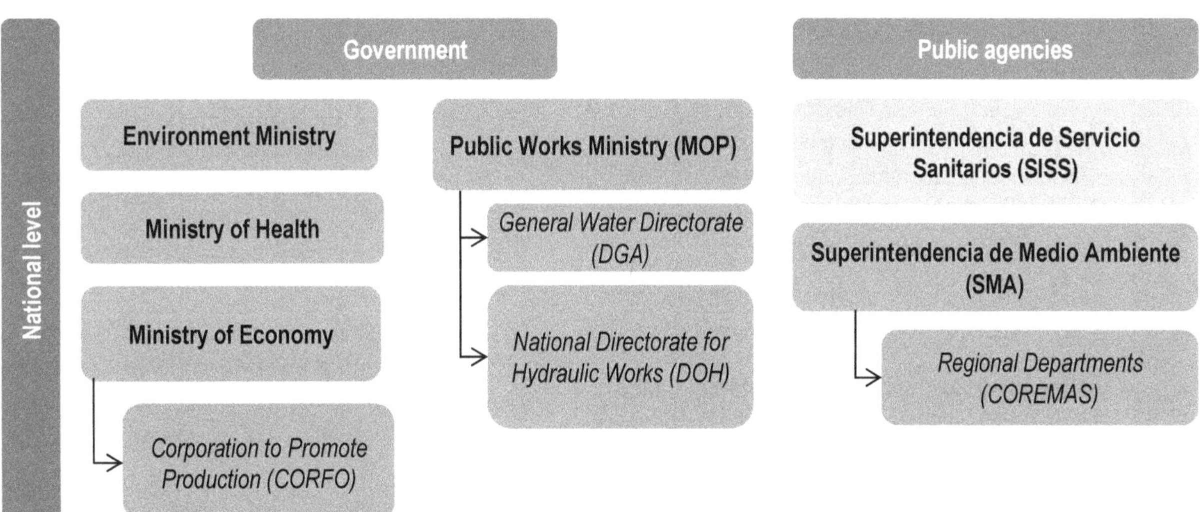

Sources: OECD Survey on the Governance of Water Regulators, 2014, OECD family database: www.oecd.org/els/family/47710686.pdf; OECD income distribution database: www.stats.oecd.org/Index.aspx?DataSetCode=IDD; OECD Statistics: http://stats.oecd.org; Superintendencia de Servicio Sanitarios (SISS): www.siss.gob.cl; IBNET: www.ib-net.org; Central Intelligence Agency: https://www.cia.gov/library/publications/the-world-factbook/index.html.

COLOMBIA

Key facts of the water sector

Territory

- Surface (km²): 1 138 910
- Population size (million): 46.582 (OECD, 2012)
- Population density (inhabitants/km²): 41 (OECD, 2012)
- Share of urban population: 75.3% of total population (CIA, 2011)
- Number of households (million): NA
- Average household size: NA

Data on the sector activity

- Number of water operators: 2 500 (OECD Survey, 2014)
- Water main networks (km pipelines): NA
- Number of active connections (million): NA
- Abstracted water volume (million m³): 2 329 (Marques, 2010)
- Average consumption (litre/resident/day): 59 (Marques, 2010)
- Non-Revenue Water (in %): 50 (IBNET, 2010)
- Turnover of the water industry (EUR): 712.4 million (Marques, 2010)

Key facts of the water regulator

- Year of establishment: 1994
- Water-specific regulator (incl. sanitation)
- Share of water operators covered: 100%
- Budget: COP 16 billion (EUR 6.3 million)
- Number of employees: 46

Source: OECD Survey, 2014.

For more information:
Regulatory Commission for Water and Sanitation (Comisión de Regulación de Agua Potable y Saneamiento Básico – CRA)
Carrera 12 N° 97-80, Piso 2, Bogotá D.C.
www.cra.gov.co
Contact: correo@cra.gov.co

Institutional arrangements for water regulation

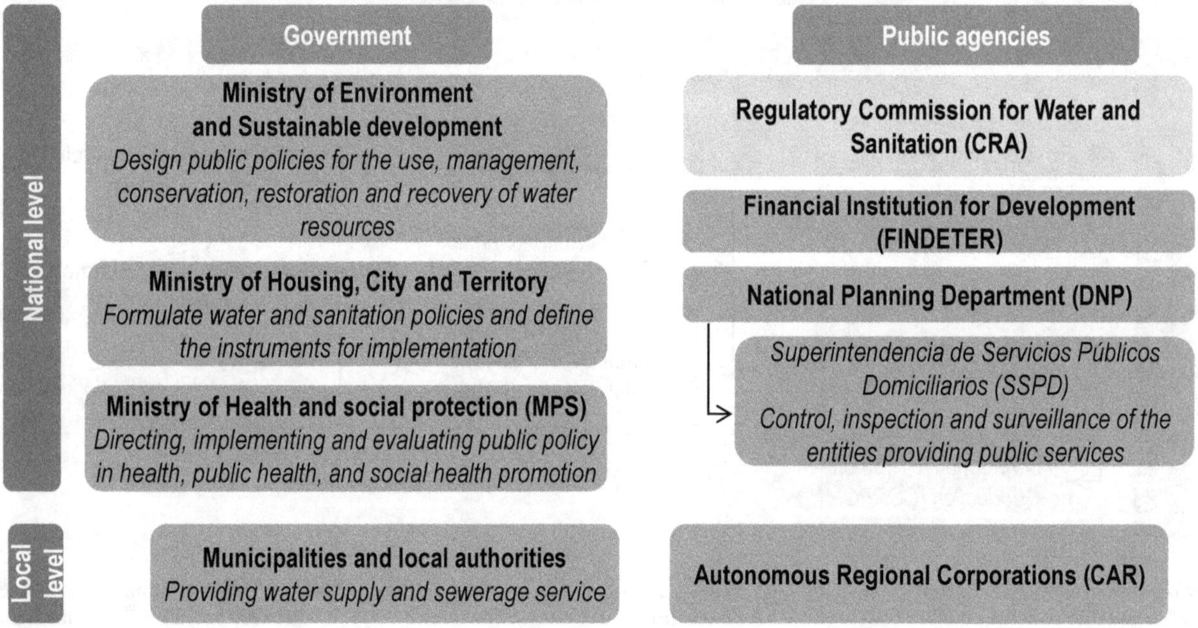

National level

Government

Ministry of Environment and Sustainable development
Design public policies for the use, management, conservation, restoration and recovery of water resources

Ministry of Housing, City and Territory
Formulate water and sanitation policies and define the instruments for implementation

Ministry of Health and social protection (MPS)
Directing, implementing and evaluating public policy in health, public health, and social health promotion

Public agencies

Regulatory Commission for Water and Sanitation (CRA)

Financial Institution for Development (FINDETER)

National Planning Department (DNP)

→ *Superintendencia de Servicios Públicos Domiciliarios (SSPD)*
Control, inspection and surveillance of the entities providing public services

Local level

Municipalities and local authorities
Providing water supply and sewerage service

Autonomous Regional Corporations (CAR)

Sources: OECD Survey on the Governance of Water Regulators, 2014, OECD Statistics: http://stats.oecd.org/; Comisión de Regulación de Agua Potable y Saneamiento Básico: www.cra.gov.co; Central Intelligence Agency: https://www.cia.gov/library/publications/the-world-factbook/index.html; Marques, R. (2010), *Regulation of Water and Wastewater Services – An International Comparison*, IWA Publishing, London.

ESTONIA

Key facts of the water sector

Territory

- Surface (km²): 45 228
- Population size (million): 1.335 (OECD, 2011)
- Population density (inhabitants/km²): 29.5 (OECD, 2011)
- Share of urban population: 69.5% of total population (CIA, 2011)
- Number of households (million): 0.597 (OECD, 2011)
- Average household size: 2.3 persons (OECD, 2011)

Data on the sector activity

- Number of water operators: 200
- Water main networks (km pipelines): N.A.
- Number of active connections (million): 1.11 (number of consumers).
- Abstracted water volume (million m³): 1 749.7 (total) / 97.6 (for water supply).
- Average consumption (litre/resident/day): 93.8 (2013)
- Non-Revenue Water (in %): N.A.
- Turnover of the water industry (EUR): 90 million (OECD Survey, 2014)

Key facts of the water regulator

- Year of establishment: 2010 (for water)
- Multi-sector regulator: water, energy (gas, electricity, district heating), railway, telecommunication (until July 2014), airport, post.
- Share of water operators covered: 35%
- Budget (EUR): 1.83 million (total)
- Number of employees:
  - Water: 5
  - Total: 60

For more information:
Estonia Competition Authority
Auna 6,
10317 Tallinn
www.konkurentsiamet.ee/?lang=en
Contact: info@konkurentsiamet.ee

Source: OECD Survey, 2014.

Institutional arrangements for water regulation

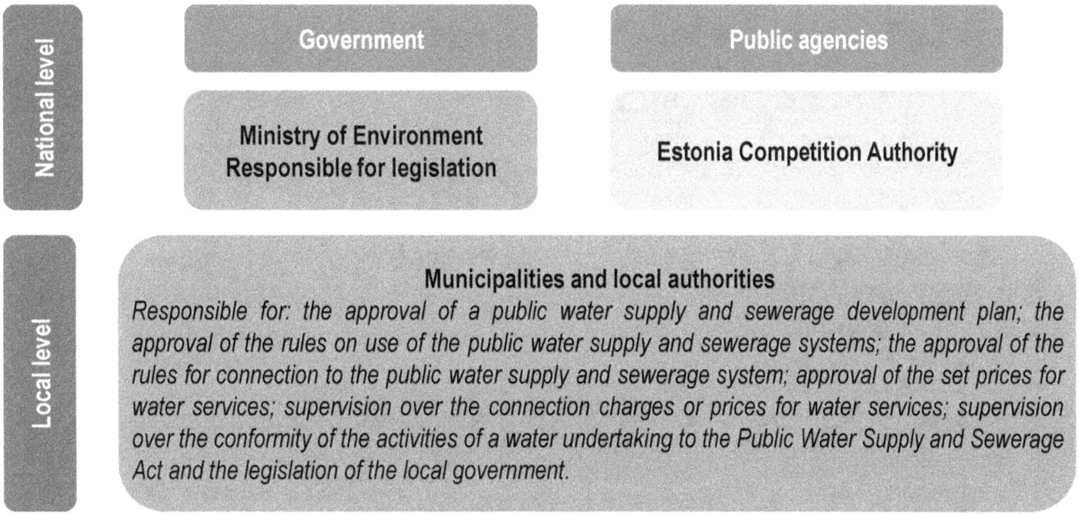

National level

Government	Public agencies
Ministry of Environment Responsible for legislation	Estonia Competition Authority

Local level

Municipalities and local authorities

Responsible for: the approval of a public water supply and sewerage development plan; the approval of the rules on use of the public water supply and sewerage systems; the approval of the rules for connection to the public water supply and sewerage system; approval of the set prices for water services; supervision over the connection charges or prices for water services; supervision over the conformity of the activities of a water undertaking to the Public Water Supply and Sewerage Act and the legislation of the local government.

Sources: OECD Survey on the Governance of Water Regulators, 2014, Estonia Competition Authority: www.konkurentsiamet.ee/?lang=en; OECD Family database: www.oecd.org/els/family/oecdfamilydatabase.htm and OECD Income Distribution Database: http://stats.oecd.org/Index.aspx?DataSetCode=IDD; Central Intelligence Agency: https://www.cia.gov/library/publications/the-world-factbook/index.html.

HUNGARY

Key facts of the water sector

Territory

- Surface (km²): 93 028
- Population size (million): 9.920 (OECD, 2012)
- Population density (inhabitants/km²): 107 (OECD, 2012)
- Share of urban population: 69.5% of total population (CIA, 2011)
- Number of households (million): 4.1 (KSH, 2011)
- Average household size: 2.6 persons (OECD, 2011)

Data on the sector activity

- Number of water operators: 47 (MEKH, 2014)
- Water main networks (km pipelines): 63 990 (drinking water pipelines)/48 744 km (waste water network) (MEKH, 2013)
- Number of active connections (million): 3.3 (MEKH, 2013)
- Abstracted water volume (million m³): 424 (MEKH, 2013)
- Average consumption (litre/resident/day): 93.15 (KSH, 2012)
- Non-Revenue Water(in %): 32 (IBNET, 2007)
- Turnover of the water industry: HUF 244 billion in 2012 (EUR 779 million) (OECD Survey, 2014)

Key facts of the water regulator

- Year of establishment: 2012 (creation of the Water Utility Supply department)
- Multi-sector regulator: Electricity, Natural Gas, District Heating, Water Utility Supply and partly Waste Management
- Share of water operators covered: 100%
- Budget: HUF 4.7 billion (total) (EUR 15 million)
- Number of employees:
  - Water: 50
  - Total: 300

For more information:
Hungarian Energy and Public Utility Regulatory Authority (MEKH)
Magyar Energetikai és Közmű-szabályozási Hivatal
1081 Budapest, II. János Pál pápa tér 7
www.mekh.hu/en/
Contact: mekh@mekh.hu

Source: OECD Survey, 2014.

Institutional arrangements for water regulation

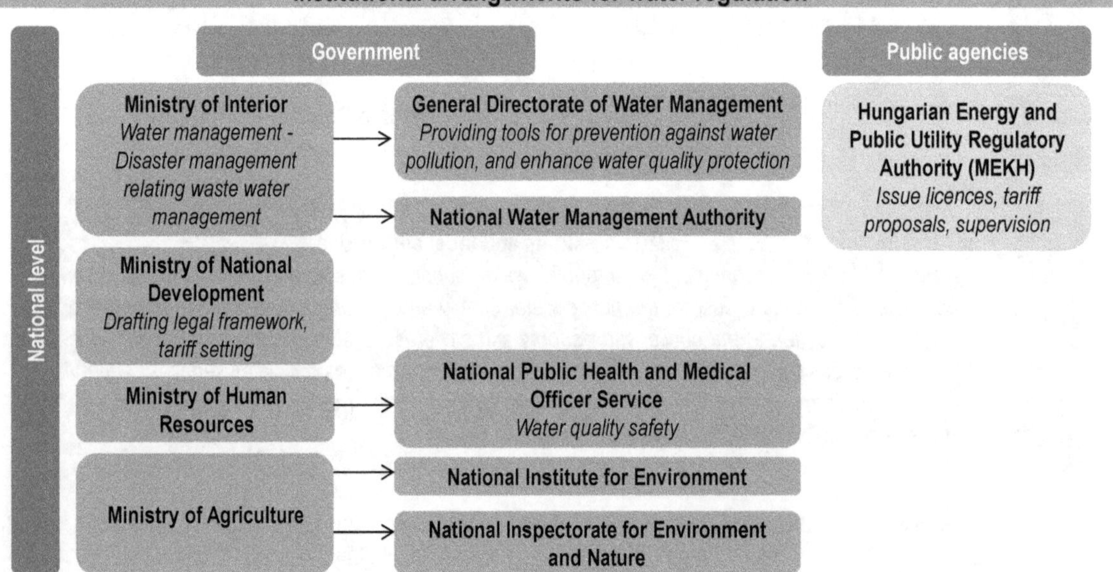

Sources: OECD Survey on the Governance of Water Regulators, 2014; MEKH: www.mekh.hu/en and written contribution received on 8 July 2014; IBNET: www.ib-net.org; OECD family database: www.oecd.org/els/family/oecdfamilydatabase.htm; KSH (Hungarian Central Statistical Office): www.ksh.hu/?lang=en; Central Intelligence Agency: https://www.cia.gov/library/publications/the-world-factbook/index.html.

INDONESIA

Key facts of the water sector

Territory

- Surface (km²): 1 904 569
- Population size (million): 247 (OECD, 2012)
- Population density (inhabitants/km²): 130 (OECD, 2012)
- Share of urban population: 50.7% of total population (CIA, 2011)
- Number of households (million): NA
- Average household size: NA

Data on the sector activity

- Number of water operators: 401 (OECD Survey, 2014)
- Water main networks (km pipelines): NA
- Number of active connections (million): NA
- Abstracted water volume (million m³): 6 600 (in 2006 – Marques, 2010)
- Average consumption (litre/resident/day): 146 (Marques, 2010)
- Non-Revenue Water (in %): 50 (Marques, 2010)
- Turnover of the water industry (EUR): 101.6 million (Marques, 2010)

Key facts of the water regulator

- Year of establishment: 2001
- Water-specific regulator (excl. sanitation)
- Share of water operators covered: 1%
- Budget: 5 to 6 billion Rupiah (EUR 320 000 to 380 000)
- Number of employees: 25

Source: OECD Survey, 2014.

For more information:
Jakarta Water Supply Regulatory Body
Badan Regulator PAM DKI Jakarta
Jl. Pejompongan No. 57
Jakarta 1021
www.brpamdki.org
www.jakartawater.org

Institutional arrangements for water regulation

National level

Government		Public agencies	Other stakeholders
Ministry of Public Works (BPPSPAM) *Establishing the standards of water service*	Ministry of Health (MoH) *Monitoring Water Quality*	National Planning Development Agency	Association of Operators (PERPAMSI)
Ministry of Home Affairs (MoHA)	Ministry of Environment *Monitoring quality standards for wastewater treatment*		Ombudsman
	Ministry for Public Housing		

Local level

Government	Public agencies	Other stakeholders
Local authorities (Governor of Jakarta)	Jakarta Water Supply Regulatory Body (JWSRB)	Jakarta Water Supply Company
Jakarta Controller Board		Water Supply Customers Committee (KPAM)

Sources: OECD Survey on the Governance of Water Regulators, 2014; OECD Statistics: http://stats.oecd.org/; Jakarta Water Supply Regulatory Body: www.jakartawater.org; IBNET: www.ib-net.org; Marques, R. (2010), *Regulation of Water and Wastewater Services – An International Comparison*, IWA Publishing, London; Central Intelligence Agency: https://www.cia.gov/library/publications/the-world-factbook/index.html.

IRELAND

Key facts of the water sector

Territory

- Surface (km²): 70 273
- Population size (million): 4.587 (OECD, 2012)
- Population density (inhabitants/km²): 65 (OECD, 2012)
- Share of urban population: 62% of total population (CIA, 2011)
- Number of households (million): 1.706 (OECD, 2011)
- Average household size: 2.9 persons (OECD, 2011)

Data on the sector activity

- Number of water operators: 1
- Water main networks (km pipelines): 25 000 (water supply network) (Department of the Environment 2012)
- Number of active connections (million): 1.31 (CER, 2014)
- Abstracted water volume (million m³): 647 (Department of the Environment 2012)
- Average consumption (litre/resident/day): 123 (Irish Water, 2014)
- Non-Revenue Water (in %): 41% (2012)
- Turnover of the water industry (EUR): not yet available

Key facts of the water regulator

- Year of establishment: 2013 (water)
- Multi-sector regulator: Electricity, gas, petroleum, energy safety and water
- Share of water operators covered: 100%
- Budget: EUR 2.3 million for 2014 (water regulation)
- Number of employees: 12 (water regulation)

For more information:
Commission for Energy Regulation (CER)
The Exchange, Belgard Square North,
Tallaght, Dublin 24
www.cer.ie
Contact: info@cer.ie

Source: OECD Survey, 2014.

Institutional arrangements for water regulation

National level

Government	Public agencies	Water operators
Department of Environment, Community and Local Government	Commission for Energy Regulation (CER)	Irish Water
	Environmental Protection Agency (EPA) *Environmental Regulation and Drinking Quality*	→ Local authorities *Operating on behalf of Irish Water as part of a service level agreement up to 2026*

Sources: OECD Survey on the Governance of Water Regulators, 2014, CER: www.cer.ie; OECD Family Database: www.oecd.org/els/family/oecdfamilydatabase.htm; OECD income distribution database: www.stats.oecd.org/Index.aspx?DataSetCode=IDD; OECD Statistics: http://stats.oecd.org; Central Intelligence Agency: https://www.cia.gov/library/publications/the-world-factbook/index.html; Department of the Environment (2012): www.environ.ie/en/PublicationsDocuments/FileDownLoad,29192,en.pdf.

ITALY

Key facts of the water sector

Territory

- Surface (km²): 301 300
- Population size (million): 59.540 (OECD, 2012)
- Population density (inhabitants/km²): 198 (OECD, 2012)
- Share of Share of urban population: 68.4% of total population (CIA, 2011)
- Number of households (million): 25.4 (OECD, 2011)
- Average household size: 2.6 persons (OECD, 2011)

Data on the sector activity

- Number of water operators: More than 2 000 (OECD Survey, 2014)
- Water main networks (km pipelines): 350 000
- Number of active connections (million): >20
- Abstracted water volume (million m³): 7 600 (Marques, 2010)
- Average consumption (litre/resident/day): 137
- Non-Revenue Water(in %): 33%
- Turnover of the water industry: EUR 8.5 billion

Key facts of the water regulator

- Year of establishment: end December 2011 (water)
- Multi-sector regulator: Electricity, gas and water
- Share of water operators covered: 100%
- Budget: EUR 44.8 million in 2012 (total)
- Number of employees: 12 (water regulation, Inspection activities are shared with electricity and gas)

For more information:
Regulatory Authority for Electricity, Gas and Water (Autorità per l'energia elettrica il gas e il sistema idrico – AEEGSI)
Piazza Cavour, 5 – 20121 Milano
www.autorita.energia.it/
Contact: info@autorita.energia.it

Source: OECD Survey, 2014.

Institutional arrangements for water regulation

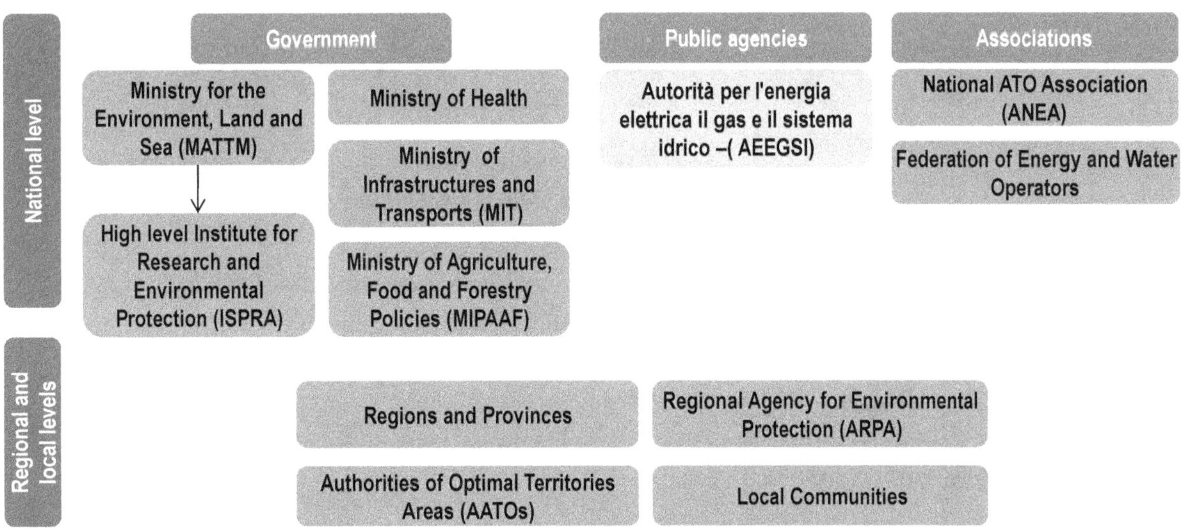

Sources: OECD Survey on the Governance of Water Regulators, 2014; OECD family database: www.oecd.org/els/family/oecdfamilydatabase.htm; OECD income distribution database: www.stats.oecd.org/Index.aspx?DataSetCode=IDD; OECD Statistics: http://stats.oecd.org; OECD (2013), *OECD Environmental Performance Reviews: Italy 2013*, OECD Publishing, Paris, http://dx.doi.org/10.1787/9789264186378-en; Central Intelligence Agency: https://www.cia.gov/library/publications/the-world-factbook/index.html and Marques, R. (2010), *Regulation of Water and Wastewater Services – An International Comparison*, IWA Publishing, London.

KOSOVO

Key facts of the water sector

Territory

- Surface (km²): 10 908
- Population size (million): 1.815 (Kosovo Agency of Statistics, 2011)
- Population density (inhabitants/km²): 177.4 (Kosovo Agency of Statistics, 2011)
- Share of urban population: 39% (Kosovo Agency of Statistics, 2011)
- Number of households (million): 0.297 (Kosovo Agency of Statistics, 2011)
- Average household size: 5.85 persons Kosovo Agency of Statistics, 2011)

Data on the sector activity

- Number of water operators: 8 (OECD Survey, 2014)
- Water main networks (km pipelines): NA
- Number of active connections (million): NA
- Abstracted water volume (million m³): 138.8 (Marques, 2010)
- Average consumption (litre/resident/day): 180 (Marques, 2010)
- Non-Revenue Water (in %): 62.5% (IBNET, 2012)
- Turnover of the water industry: EUR 25 million (OECD Survey, 2014)

Key facts of the water regulator

- Year of establishment: 2004
- Water-specific regulator (incl. sanitation)
- Share of water operators covered: 100%
- Budget: EUR 359 000 (for 2014)
- Number of employees: 19

Source: OECD Survey, 2014.

For more information:
Water and Wastewater Regulatory Office of Kosovo (WWRO)
Ferat Dragaj str. No:68
Sunny Hill
Prishtina
Contact: lule.aliu@wwro-ks.org

Institutional arrangements for water regulation

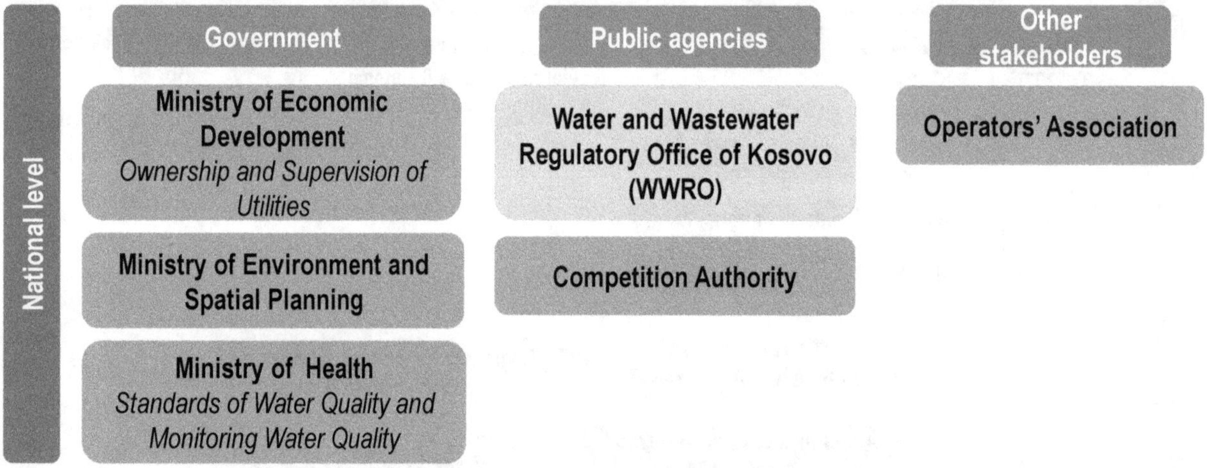

National level

Government	Public agencies	Other stakeholders
Ministry of Economic Development *Ownership and Supervision of Utilities*	**Water and Wastewater Regulatory Office of Kosovo (WWRO)**	**Operators' Association**
Ministry of Environment and Spatial Planning	**Competition Authority**	
Ministry of Health *Standards of Water Quality and Monitoring Water Quality*		

Sources: OECD Survey on the Governance of Water Regulators, 2014, WWRO: www.wwro-ks.org; IBNET: www.ib-net.org; Kosovo Agency of Statistics, Census 2011: www.ask.rks-gov.net/eng; Marques, R. (2010), *Regulation of Water and Wastewater Services – An International Comparison*, IWA Publishing, London.

LATVIA

Key facts of the water sector

Territory

- Surface (km²): 64 589
- Population size (million): 2.001 (Central Statistical Bureau (CSB), est. 2014)
- Population density (inhabitants/km²): 31 (CSB, est. 2014)
- Share of urban population: 68% of total population (CSB, 2013)
- Number of households (million): 0.82 (CSB, 2013)
- Average household size: 2.43 persons

Data on the sector activity

- Number of water operators: 160 (OECD Survey, 2014)
- Water main networks (km pipelines): 4 856 km (PUC, based on data submitted by enterprises for 2012)
- Number of active connections (million): 1.266 active contracts in 2012 (PUC)
- Abstracted water volume (million m³): 81.5 (Latvian Environment, Geology and Meteorology Centre)
- Average consumption (litre/resident/day): 100 (PUC)
- Non-Revenue Water (in %): 24 (average water losses, PUC)
- Turnover of the water industry: EUR 87 million (OECD Survey, 2014)

Key facts of the water regulator

- Year of establishment: 2001 (water from 2009)
- Multi-sector regulator: energy, telecommunications, post, railway transport, district heating, waste disposal and water management
- Share of water operators covered: 100%
- Budget: EUR 5 018 529 in 2013 (total)
- Number of employees:
  - Water: 8 in the municipal services department
  - Total: 123 (including 5 commissioners)

For more information:
Public Utilities Commission of Latvia (PUC)
45 Unijas street,
Riga
www.sprk.gov.lv/
Contact: sprk@sprk.gov.lv

Source: OECD Survey, 2014.

Institutional arrangements for water regulation

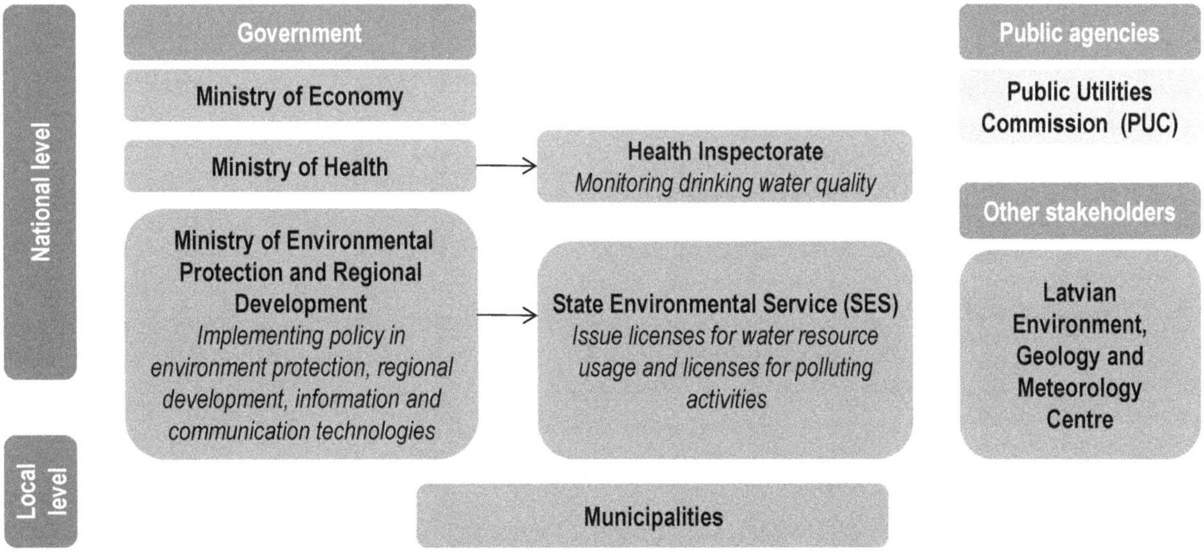

National level

Government

- Ministry of Economy
- Ministry of Health → Health Inspectorate: *Monitoring drinking water quality*
- Ministry of Environmental Protection and Regional Development: *Implementing policy in environment protection, regional development, information and communication technologies* → State Environmental Service (SES): *Issue licenses for water resource usage and licenses for polluting activities*

Public agencies

- Public Utilities Commission (PUC)

Other stakeholders

- Latvian Environment, Geology and Meteorology Centre

Local level

- Municipalities

Sources: OECD Survey on the Governance of Water Regulators, 2014; Public Utilities Commission: www.sprk.gov.lv; IBNET: www.ib-net.org; Latvia Central Bureau of Statistics: www.csb.gov.lv/en/statistikas-temas/population-key-indicators-30624.html; Central Intelligence Agency: https://www.cia.gov/library/publications/the-world-factbook/index.html.

MALAYSIA

Key facts of the water sector

Territory

- Surface (km²): 329 847
- Population size (million): 28.3 (Department of Statistics, 2010)
- Population density (inhabitants/km²): 86.7 (Department of Statistics, 2010)
- Share of urban population: 72.8% of total population (CIA, 2011)
- Number of households (million): 6.34 (Department of Statistics, 2010)
- Average household size: 4.2 persons (Department of Statistics, 2010)

Data on the sector activity

- Number of water operators: 847 (12 individual licenses/public operators and 835 class licences/ private operators; OECD Survey, 2014)
- Water main networks (km pipelines): 138 669
- Number of active connections (million): 6.833 (SPAN, 2012)
- Abstracted water volume (million m³): 6 153
- Average consumption (litre/resident/day): 210
- Non-Revenue Water (in %): 36.4 (SPAN, 2012)
- Turnover of the water industry: MYR 4.5 billion (EUR 1.03 billion – OECD Survey, 2014)

Key facts of the water regulator

- Year of establishment: 2007
- Water-specific regulator (incl. sanitation)
- Share of water operators covered: 100%
- Budget: MYR 32 million (EUR 7.4 million)
- Number of employees: 192 (incl. 66 non-executive and non-technical)

For more information:
National Water Services Commission (SPAN)
Ground and 1st Floor, Prima Avenue 7, Block 3510,
Jalan Teknokrat 6,
63000 Cyberjaya, Malaysia
Contact: span@span.gov.my

Source: OECD Survey, 2014.

Institutional arrangements for water regulation

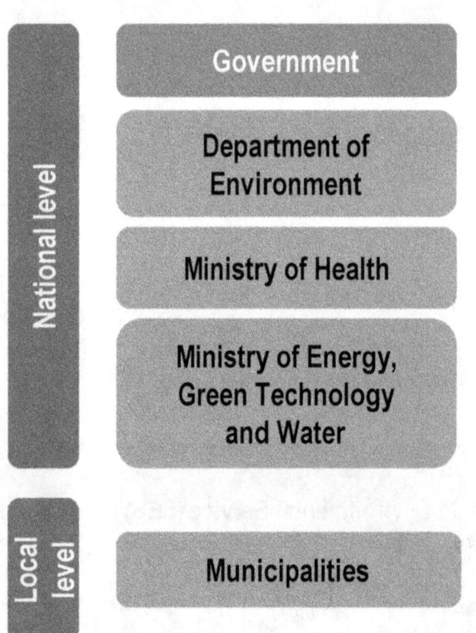

Sources: OECD Survey on the Governance of Water Regulators, 2014, IBNET: www.ib-net.org; SPAN: www.span.gov.my; Department of Statistics Malaysia: www.statistics.gov.my/portal/index.php?option=com_content&view=section&id=21&Itemid=154&lang=en; Central Intelligence Agency: https://www.cia.gov/library/publications/the-world-factbook/index.html.

MOZAMBIQUE

Key facts of the water sector

Territory

- Surface (km²): 799 380
- Population size (million): 25.8 (WB, 2013)
- Population density (inhabitants/km²): 32 (WB, 2013)
- Share of urban population: 31% of total population (CIA, 2011)
- Number of households (million): 5.16 (CRA, 2014)
- Average household size: 5 persons (CRA, 2014)

Data on the sector activity

- Number of water operators: 15 (over 500 informal small operators) (OECD Survey, 2014)
- Water main networks (km pipelines): 7 600 (CRA, 2014)
- Number of active connections (million): 0.44 (CRA, 2014)
- Abstracted water volume (million m³): 141 (CRA, 2014)
- Average consumption (litre/resident/day): 76 (domestic) (CRA, 2014)
- Non-Revenue Water (in %): 43 (CRA, 2014)
- Turnover of the water industry: MZM 2 200 million (EUR 56.7 million) (CRA, 2014)

Key facts of the water regulator

- Year of establishment: 2000
- Water-specific regulator (incl. sanitation)
- Share of water operators covered: 100% of formal operators
- Budget: MZM 24 million (EUR 570 000)
- Number of employees: 65 (35 employees, 20 technical staff, and 10 part-time local agents)

For more information:
Conselho de Regulação de Águas (CRA)
Av. Amilcar Cabral, 757
C. Postal 235 – Maputo
Mozambique
www.cra.org.mz
Contact: info@cra.org.mz

Source: OECD Survey, 2014.

Institutional arrangements for water regulation

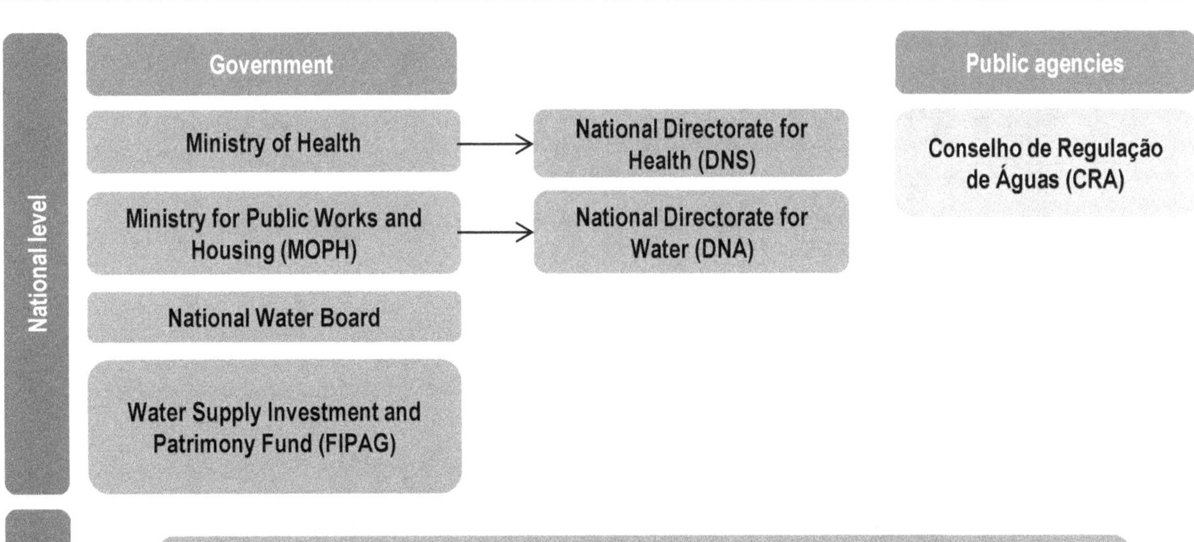

Sources: OECD Survey on the Governance of Water Regulators, 2014, CRA: www.cra.org.mz; IBNET: www.ib-net.org; World Bank: http://data.worldbank.org/country/mozambique; Central Intelligence Agency: https://www.cia.gov/library/publications/the-world factbook/index.html and Marques, R. (2010), *Regulation of Water and Wastewater Services – An International Comparison*, IWA Publishing, London.

PERU

Key facts of the water sector

Territory

- Surface (km²): 1 285 216
- Population size (million): 30.8
- Population density (in habitants/km²): 24
- Share of urban population: 76%
- Number of households (million): 8
- Average household size: 4 persons

Source: National Institute of Statistics and Information of Peru (2013).

Data on the sector activity

- Number of water operators: 50 (OECD Survey, 2014)
- Water main networks (km pipelines): 31 426 (SUNASS, 2013)
- Number of active connections (million): 3 (SUNASS, 2013)
- Abstracted water volume (million m³): 1 358 (SUNASS, 2013)
- Average consumption (litre/resident/day): 156 (SUNASS, 2013)
- Non-Revenue Water (in %): 36% (SUNASS, 2013)
- Turnover of the water industry: 2.6 billion Nuevos Soles (EUR 706 million) (OECD Survey, 2014)

Key facts of the water regulator

- Year of establishment: 1992
- Water-specific regulator (incl. sanitation)
- Share of water operators covered: 100% urban operators
- Budget: 26 million Nuevos Soles (€7.1 million)
- Number of employees: 192

Source: OECD Survey, 2014.

For more information:
Superintendencia Nacional de Servicios de Saneamiento – SUNASS
Address: Av. Bernardo Monteagudo N° 210
Lima 17
Website: www.sunass.gob.pe
Contact: gpn@sunass.gob.pe

Institutional arrangements for water regulation

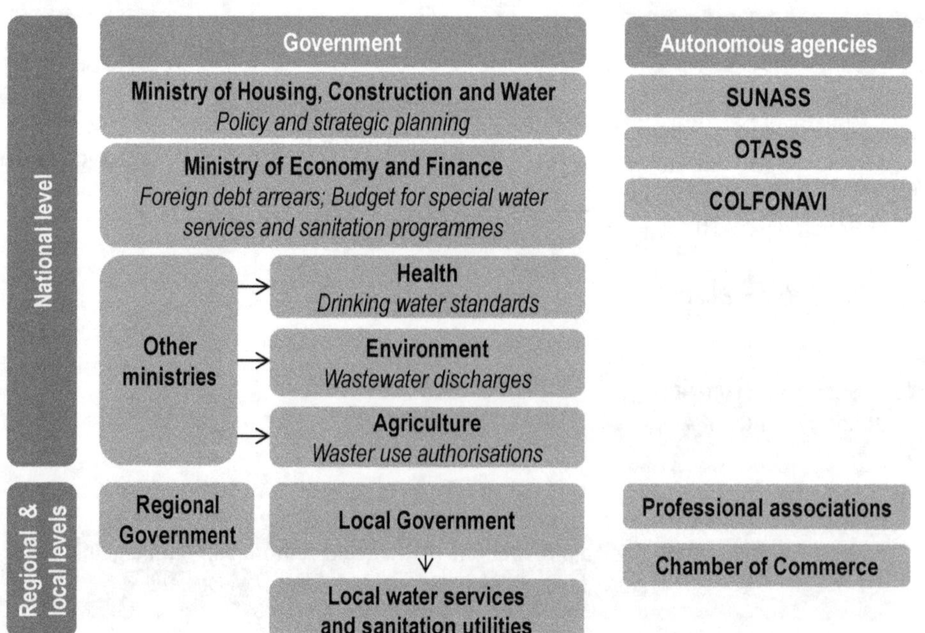

Sources: OECD Survey on the Governance of Water Regulators, 2014; National Institute of Statistics and Information of Peru (2013); SUNASS (2013) and World (2010), "Local Financing of Water Utilities: Challenges and Opportunities – The Case of Peru", http://documents.worldbank.org/curated/en/2010/06/12731770/local-financing-water-utilities-challenges-opportunities-case-peru.

PORTUGAL

Key facts of the water sector

Territory

- Surface (km²): 92 300
- Population size (million): 10.637 (OECD, 2011)
- Population density (inhabitants/km²): 115 (OECD, 2011)
- Share of urban population: 61.1% of total population (CIA, 2011)
- Number of households (million): 4.042 (OECD, 2011)
- Average household size: 2.8 persons (OECD, 2011)

Data on the sector activity

- Number of water operators: 478 (ERSAR, 2014)
- Water main networks (km pipelines): 101 213 (in 2012; ERSAR, 2014)
- Number of active connections (million): 4.502 (number of clients served in 2012; ERSAR, 2014)
- Abstracted water volume (million m³): 818 (in 2012; ERSAR, 2014)
- Average consumption (litre/resident/day): 195 (ERSAR, 2014)
- Non-Revenue Water (in %): 31% (ERSAR, 2014)
- Turnover of the water industry: EUR 1 730 million (for water and sanitation in 2012; ERSAR, 2014)

Key facts of the water regulator

- Year of establishment: 1999
- Multi-sector regulator: drinking water, sanitation and waste management services
- Share of water operators covered: 100%
- Budget: EUR 8 million in 2013 (total)
- Number of employees: 77 (total, incl. 21 administrative staff and 24 staff for audits and inspections)

For more information:
The Water and Waste Services Regulation Authority (ERSAR)
Centro Empresarial Torres de Lisboa
Rua Tomás da Fonseca, Torre G – 8º
1600-209 Lisbon
www.ersar.pt/website/
Contact: geral@ersar.pt

Source: OECD Survey, 2014.

Institutional arrangements for water regulation

National level

Government

Ministry for Environment and Energy (MAOTE)
Policy definition and strategy; ownership of bulk services

Public agencies

Water and waste services regulation authority (ERSAR)

Portuguese Environmental Agency (APA)
Water planning; water abstraction and discharge licensing

Competition Authority (AdC)
Enforcement of competition rules

Operator's association

Local level

Municipalities
Decision about retail tariffs; ownership of retail services

Sources: OECD Survey on the Governance of Water Regulators, 2014, ERSAR: www.ersar.pt/website_en and written contribution received on 4th July 2014; OECD Family Database: www.oecd.org/els/family/oecdfamilydatabase.htm; OECD income distribution database: www.stats.oecd.org/Index.aspx?DataSetCode=IDD; OECD Statistics: http://stats.oecd.org/Index.aspx?DataSetCode=RPOP; Central Intelligence Agency: https://www.cia.gov/library/publications/the-world-factbook/index.html and Marques, R. (2010), *Regulation of Water and Wastewater Services – An International Comparison*, IWA Publishing, London.

ROMANIA

Key facts of the water sector

Territory

- Surface (km²): 238 391
- Population size (million): 20 (Eurostat, 2013)
- Population density (inhabitants/km²): 84 (Eurostat, 2013)
- Share of urban population: 53% of total population (CIA, 2011)
- Number of households (million): NA
- Average household size: 2.8 persons (OECD, 2011)

Data on the sector activity

- Number of water operators: 1 077 in 2013 (OECD Survey, 2014)
- Water main networks (km pipelines): 42 000 (Marques, 2010)
- Number of active connections (million): NA
- Abstracted water volume (million m³): NA
- Average consumption (litre/resident/day): 200 approx. (Marques, 2010)
- Non-Revenue Water (in %): 42.8% (IBNET, 2010)
- Turnover of the water industry: LEI 15 367 713 (EUR 3.4 million, OECD Survey, 2014)

Key facts of the water regulator

- Year of establishment: 2002
- Multi-sector regulator: water and wastewater, transport, district heating, sanitation, public lighting.
- Share of water operators covered: 100%
- Budget: LEI 5.166 million in total (EUR 1.1 million)
- Number of employees: 95 in total (excl. 1 president and 1 vice-president)

For more information:
National Regulatory Authority for Municipal Services (ANRSC)
Str. Stavropoleos nr.6, Sector 3,
Bucuresti
www.anrsc.ro
Contact: biroupresa@anrsc.ro

Source: OECD Survey, 2014.

Institutional arrangements for water regulation

	Government	Public agencies	Other stakeholders
National level	Ministry of Regional Development and Public Administration (MRDPA) *Government decisions regarding changing legislations*	National Regulatory Authority for Municipal Services (ANRSC)	Authority for Customer Protection
	Ministry of the Environment and Water	Competition Authority	Romanian Water Association (ARA)
	Ministry for Public Health (MSP)		
Local level	Municipalities		
	Regional Inspectorate of Environment and Water		

Sources: OECD Survey on the Governance of Water Regulators, 2014, ANRSC: www.anrsc.ro; OECD Family Database: www.oecd.org/els/family/oecdfamilydatabase.htm; Central Intelligence Agency: https://www.cia.gov/library/publications/the-world-factbook/index.html; IBNET: www.ib-net.org; Eurostat: http://epp.eurostat.ec.europa.eu/tgm/table.do?tab=table&language=en&pcode=tps00001&tableSelection=1&footnotes=yes&labeling=labels&plugin=1.

UKRAINE

Key facts of the water sector

Territory

- Surface (km²): 603 550
- Population size (million): 45.49 (WB, 2013)
- Population density (inhabitants/km²): 75 (WB, 2013)
- Share of urban population: 69% of total population (CIA, 2011)
- Number of households (million): 16.959 (2013)
- Average household size: 2.58 persons (2013)

Data on the sector activity

- Number of water operators: 1 595 (OECD Survey, 2014)
- Water main networks (km pipelines): 78 661 (2013)
- Number of active connections (million): 30.1 (2013)
- Abstracted water volume (million m³): 2 913 (2013)
- Average consumption (litre/resident/day): 130 (2013)
- Non-Revenue Water (in %): 44 (IBNET, 2007)
- Turnover of the water industry: UAH 10 billion (EUR 629 million – OECD Survey, 2014)

Key facts of the water regulator

- Year of establishment: 2011
- Multi-sector regulator: District heating, water supply and sanitation and solid waste
- Share of water operators covered: 9.4% (150 water operators which in total cover 92 % of all output water supply and sewerage services)
- Budget: UAH 40 million (total) (EUR 2.54 million)
- Number of employees: 61 (water regulation)

Source: OECD Survey, 2014.

For more information:
The National Commission of the State Public Utilities Regulation
Dymytrova str. 24,
Kyiv, 03150
www.nkp.gov.ua/en/scms/view/326
Contact: list@nkp.gov.ua

Institutional arrangements for water regulation

National level

Government

Ministry of Economic Development and Trade
Responsible for policy of economic and social development, external economic policies and security of consumer rights. Monitoring price setting policy

Ministry of Ecology and Natural Resources
Monitoring environment protection and supervision of the drinking water resources

Ministry for Regional Development, Building and Housing
Responsible for policy in building, housing, communal services, architecture and urban development

Ministry of Health
Responsible for regulatory policy of health care, sanitary and epidemiological welfare of the population. Monitoring drinking water quality

Public agencies

The National commission of the state public utilities regulation of Ukraine

Anti-Monopoly Committee
Protection of economic competition

Local authorities / Local self-government
Regulation, supervision and control over the systems of water distribution and over the quality of drinking water (local level)

Sources: OECD Survey on the Governance of Water Regulators, 2014, The National Commission of the State Public Utilities Regulation: www.nkp.gov.ua/en/scms/view/326; World Bank: www.data.worldbank.org/country/ukraine; IBNET: www.ib-net.org; Central Intelligence Agency: https://www.cia.gov/library/publications/the-world-factbook/index.html.

UNITED KINGDOM/ENGLAND AND WALES

Key facts of the water sector

Territory

- Surface (km²): 156 200
- Population size (million): 56.6 (ONS, 2012)
- Population density (inhabitants/km²): 362 (ONS, 2012)
- Share of urban population: 76.3% of total population, 2010 (OECD, 2012)
- Number of households (million): 26.4 (UK – ONS, 2010)
- Average household size: 2.37 persons (UK – ONS, 2013)

Data on the sector activity

- Number of water operators: 18 (OECD Survey, 2014)
- Water main networks (km pipelines): 339 000
- Number of active connections (million): 24+
- Abstracted water volume (million m³): 5 469 (2007 in Marques, 2010)
- Average consumption (litre/resident/day): 147 (Marques, 2010)
- Non-Revenue Water (in %): 22 (Marques, 2010)
- Turnover of the water industry: GBP 11 billion (EUR 13 billion – OECD Survey, 2014)

Key facts of the water regulator

- Year of establishment: 1989
- Water-specific regulator (incl. sanitation)
- Share of water operators covered: 100%
- Budget: GBP 20 million (EUR 24 million)
- Number of employees: 175

For more information:
Water Service Regulatory Authority (OFWAT)
Centre City Tower, 7 Hill Street
Birmingham B5 4UA, United Kingdom
www.ofwat.gov.uk
Contact: mailbox@ofwat.gsi.gov.uk

Source: OECD Survey, 2014.

Institutional arrangements for water regulation

	Government of England	Government of Wales	Public agencies (E&W)	Other stakeholders (E&W)
Central level	**Department for Environment, Food and Rural Affairs (DEFRA)** *Environment regulation*	**Welsh Government**	**Regulatory Commission for Water and Sanitation (OFWAT)**	**Consumer Council for Water (CCW)**
	Secretary of State for Environment, Food and Rural Affairs (SSEFRA)	**Natural Resources Wales** *Environmental regulation*	**Environment Agency (EA)** *Environmental regulation*	**Operator's Association (WaterUK)**
		Natural Assembly for Wales	**Competition and Markets Authority (CMA)**	
			Drinking Water Inspectorate (DWI) *Drinking water quality*	

Sources: OECD Survey on the Governance of Water Regulators, 2014; OFWAT: www.ofwat.gov.uk; Marques, R. (2010), *Regulation of Water and Wastewater Services – An International Comparison*, IWA Publishing, London; ONS: www.ons.gov.uk/ons/datasets-and-tables/index.html?pageSize=50&sortBy=none&sortDirection=none&newquery=average+household+size&content-type=Reference+table&content-type=Dataset and www.ons.gov.uk/ons/rel/pop-estimate/population-estimates-for-uk--england-and-wales--scotland-and-northern-ireland/mid-2001-to-mid-2010-revised/index.html; Elaborations on the metropolitan database, OECD (2012), *Redefining "Urban": A New Way to Measure Metropolitan Areas*, OECD Publishing, Paris, http://dx.doi.org/10.1787/9789264174108-en.

UNITED KINGDOM/NORTHERN IRELAND

Key facts of the water sector

Territory

- Surface (km²): 13 600 (ONS, 2012)
- Population size (million): 1.8 (ONS, 2012)
- Population density (inhabitants/km²): 133 (ONS, 2012)
- Share of urban population: 64% (ONS, 2012)
- Number of households (million): 0.74 (NISRA, 2010)
- Average household size: 2.47 persons (NISRA, 2010)

Data on the sector activity

- Number of water operators: 1 (OECD Survey, 2014)
- Water main networks (km pipelines): 26 700 (NI Water 2013/14)
- Number of active connections (million): 0.8 (NI Water 2013/14)
- Abstracted water volume (million m³): 226 (Marques, 2010)
- Average consumption (litre/resident/day): 266 (Marques, 2010)
- Non-Revenue Water (in %): 27% (Marques, 2010)
- Turnover of the water industry: GBP 367 million (EUR 462 million – OECD Survey, 2014)

Key facts of the water regulator

- Year of establishment: 2007 (water)
- Multi-sector regulator: Electricity, gas and water
- Share of water operators covered: 100%
- Budget: GBP 1.4 million (EUR 1.76 million) (total)
- Number of employees: 10 (water)

Source: OECD Survey, 2014.

For more information:
Northern Ireland Authority for Utility Regulator (NIAUR)
Queen's House, 14 Queen Street
Belfast, BT1 6ED, Northern Ireland
www.uregni.gov.uk
Contact: info@uregni.gov.uk

Institutional arrangements for water regulation

	Government	Public agencies	Other stakeholders
Central level	**Northern Ireland Assembly and Executive** *The Executive's policy is to maintain quality levels, deliver affordable service improvements in key customer areas and promote a sustainable water industry*	**Northern Ireland Authority for Utility Regulator (NIAUR)**	**Consumer Council for Northern Ireland**
	Department for Regional Development (DRD) *Policy on water & sewerage services. Management of the Department's shareholder interest in Northern Ireland Water*	**Northern Ireland Environment Agency (NIEA)** *Environmental regulator - Protect and improve the environment*	**Northern Ireland Water** *Provider of water and sewerage services in Northern Ireland*
		Drinking Water Inspectorate (DWI) *Monitoring the quality of drinking water*	**Operator's Association (WaterUK)**
		Competition and Markets Authority	

Sources: OECD Survey on the Governance of Water Regulators, 2014; ONS (2012): www.ons.gov.uk/ons/dcp171780_275448.pdf;
NISRA (2010): www.nisra.gov.uk/archive/demography/population/household/NI08_House_Projs.pdf;
NI Water (2013/14): www.niwater.com/sitefiles/resources/pdf/reports/annualreport/niwannualreport2013-14.pdf.

UNITED KINGDOM/SCOTLAND

Key facts of the water sector

Territory

- Surface (km²): 78 387
- Population size (million): 5.327 (NRS, est. 2013)
- Population density (inhabitants/km²): 68 (NRS, est. 2013)
- Share of urban population: 51.8% of total population, 2010 (OECD, 2012)
- Number of households (million): 2.373 (NRS, 2011)
- Average household size: 2.19 persons (NRS, 2011)

Data on the sector activity

- Number of water operators: 15 (1 national supplier and 14 licensed non-household retailers – OECD Survey, 2014)
- Water main networks (km pipelines): 48 164 (WISC, 2014)
- Number of active connections (million): 2.61 (WISC, 2014)
- Abstracted water volume (million m³): 838 (Marques, 2010)
- Average consumption (litre/resident/day): 150 (Scottish Water, 2011)
- Non-Revenue Water (in %): 37% (Marques, 2010)
- Turnover of the water industry: GBP 1 055.505 million, revenue of the national supplier (EUR 1 323 million, OECD Survey, 2014)

Key facts of the water regulator

- Year of establishment: 2005
- Water-specific regulator (incl. sanitation)
- Share of water operators covered: 100%
- Budget: GBP 2.04 million, excl. levy on licences operators (EUR 2.54 million)
- Number of employees: 17 (excl. 3 Commission members)

For more information:
Water Industry Commission for Scotland (WISC)
First Floor – Moray House
Forthside Way
Stirling
FK8 1QZ – Scotland
www.watercommission.co.uk/
Contact: enquiries@watercommission.co.uk

Source: OECD Survey, 2014.

Institutional arrangements for water regulation

Level	Government	Public agencies	Other stakeholders
Central level	**Scottish Government** *Set principles of charging and agree investment objectives for public health and the environment*	**Water Industry Commission for Scotland (WICS)**	**Citizens Advice Scotland** *Independent consumer advice network*
Central level		**Drinking Water Quality Regulator for Scotland (DWQR)** *Monitoring the quality of drinking water*	
Central level		**Scottish Environment Protection Agency (SEPA)** *Scotland's environmental regulator - Protect and improve the environment*	
Central level		**Scottish Public Service Ombudsman** *Consumer protection and dispute resolution*	
Local level	**Local authorities** *Private supplies*		

Sources: OECD Survey on the Governance of Water Regulators, 2014, WISC: www.watercommission.co.uk; National Records of Scotland, 2011 Census data: www.nrscotland.gov.uk/news/2014/scotlands-population-at-its-highest-ever; Scotland Government: www.scotland.gov.uk/resource/buildingstandards/2013Domestic/chunks/ch04s28.html and www.scotlandscensus.gov.uk/news/release-1b-now-published; IBNET: www.ib-net.org; Marques, R. (2010), *Regulation of Water and Wastewater Services – An International Comparison*, IWA Publishing, London Elaborations on the metropolitan database; and OECD (2012), *Redefining "Urban": A New Way to Measure Metropolitan Areas*, OECD Publishing, Paris, http://dx.doi.org/10.1787/9789264174108-en.

UNITED STATES/HAWAII

Key facts of the water sector

Territory

- Surface (km²): 28 311 (US Census Bureau, 2010)
- Population size (million): 1.404 (US Census Bureau, 2013 est.)
- Population density (inhabitants/km²): 83 (US Census Bureau, 2010)
- Share of urban population: not available
- Number of households (million): 0.447 (US Census Bureau, 2008-2012)
- Average household size: 2.95 persons (US Census Bureau, 2008-2012)

Data on the sector activity

- Number of water operators: 130 (OECD Survey, 2014)
- Water main networks (km pipelines): NA
- Number of active connections (million): NA
- Abstracted water volume (million m³): NA
- Average consumption (litre/resident/day): 660 for the United States (Marques, 2010)
- Non-Revenue Water (in %): NA
- Turnover of the water industry (EUR): NA

Key facts of the water regulator

- Year of establishment: 1913
- Multi-sector regulator: Electricity, Gas, Water, Wastewater, Motor Carrier Transportation, Water Carrier Transportation, Telecommunication
- Share of water operators covered: 18%
- Budget: USD 6 million (total) (EUR 4.3 million)
- Number of employees: 40 (total, no dedicated staff for water)

For more information:
Hawaii Public Utilities Commission
465 South King Street,
#103 Honolulu,
Hawaii 96813
www.puc.hawaii.gov
Contact: hawaii.puc@hawaii.gov

Source: OECD Survey, 2014.

Institutional arrangements for water regulation

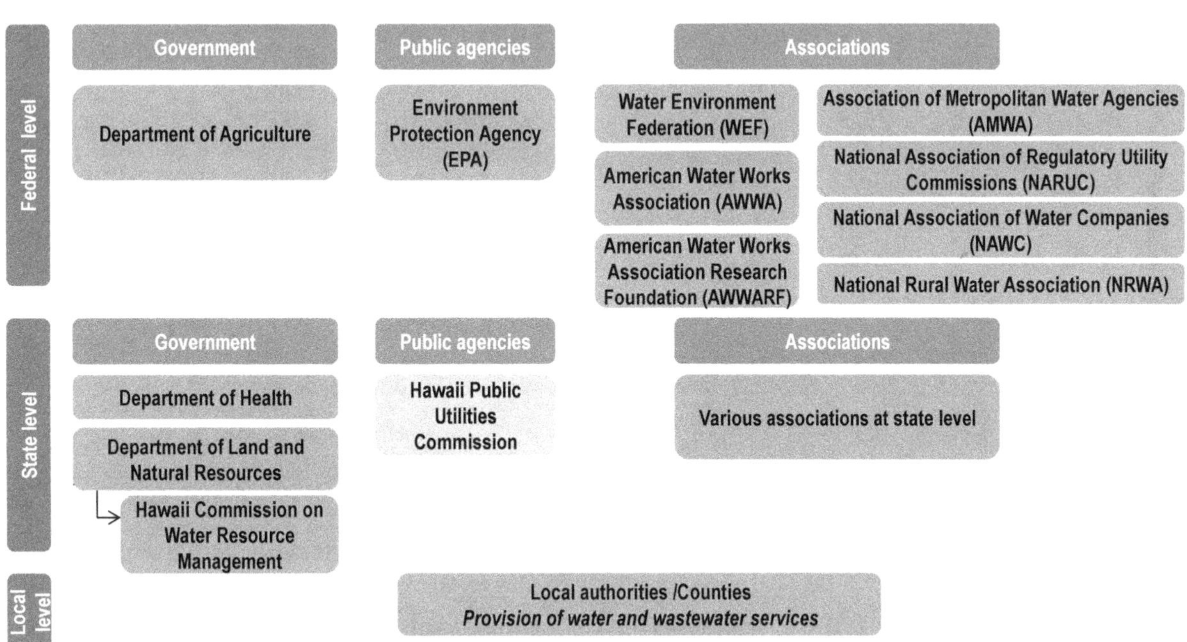

Sources: OECD Survey on the Governance of Water Regulators, 2014, Hawaii Public Utilities Commission: www.puc.hawaii.gov and Special Fund Report: http://puc.hawaii.gov/wp-content/uploads/2013/04/FY-2012-HI-PUC-Special-Fund-Report.pdf; US Census Bureau: http://quickfacts.census.gov/qfd/states/15000.html; and Marques, R. (2010), *Regulation of Water and Wastewater Services – An International Comparison*, IWA Publishing, London.

UNITED STATES/MAINE

Key facts of the water sector

Territory

- Surface (km²): 91 646 (US Census Bureau, 2010)
- Population size (million): 1.328 (US Census Bureau, 2013 est.)
- Population density (inhabitants/km²): 17 (US Census Bureau, 2010)
- Share of urban population: 14.6% of total population, 2010 (OECD, 2012)
- Number of households (million): 0.553 (US Census Bureau, 2008-2012)
- Average household size: 2.34 persons (US Census Bureau, 2008-2012)

Data on the sector activity

- Number of water operators: 150 drinking water systems (OECD Survey, 2014)
- Water main networks (km pipelines): NA
- Number of active connections (million): NA
- Abstracted water volume (million m³): NA
- Average consumption (litre/resident/day): 660 for the United States (Marques, 2010)
- Non-Revenue Water (in %): NA
- Turnover of the water industry: USD 131 million, revenues of all water utilities (EUR 96 million – OECD Survey, 2014)

Key facts of the water regulator

- Year of establishment: 1915
- Multi-sector regulator: Electricity, telephone, gas, drinking water (not sewerage) and ferry service
- Share of water operators covered: 100% of drinking water systems
- Budget:
  - USD 500 000 (revenues collected from water utilities) (EUR 364 545)
  - USD 6.4 million (total) (EUR 4.7 million)
- Number of employees: 4 (water regulation)

For more information:
Maine Public Utilities Commission
18 State House Station
Augusta, ME 04333-0018
www.maine.gov/mpuc
Contact: maine.puc@maine.gov

Source: OECD Survey, 2014.

Institutional arrangements for water regulation

Federal level

- Government: Department of Agriculture
- Public agencies: Environment Protection Agency (EPA)
- Associations: Water Environment Federation (WEF); American Water Works Association (AWWA); American Water Works Association Research Foundation (AWWARF); Association of Metropolitan Water Agencies (AMWA); National Association of Regulatory Utility Commissions (NARUC); National Association of Water Companies (NAWC); National Rural Water Association (NRWA)

State level

- Government: Maine Department of Environmental Protection; Maine Department of Health and Human Resources → Drinking Water Programme
- Public agencies: Maine Public Utilities Commission
- Associations: Various associations at state level

Local level

- Local authorities / Counties — *Provision of water and wastewater services*

Sources: OECD Survey on the Governance of Water Regulators, 2014, Maine Public Utilities Commission: www.maine.gov/mpuc; US Census Bureau: http://quickfacts.census.gov/qfd/states/23000.html; "Elaborations on the metropolitan database"; OECD (2012), *Redefining "Urban": A New Way to Measure Metropolitan Areas*, OECD Publishing, Paris, http://dx.doi.org/10.1787/9789264174108-en; and Marques, R. (2010), *Regulation of Water and Wastewater Services – An International Comparison*, IWA Publishing, London.

UNITED STATES/OHIO

Key facts of the water sector

Territory

- Surface (km²): 116 096
- Population size (million): 11.571 (US Census Bureau, 2013 est.)
- Population density (inhabitants/km²): 109 (US Census Bureau, 2013 est.)
- Share of urban population: 62.3% of total population, 2010 (OECD, 2012)
- Number of households (million): 4.556 (US Census Bureau, 2008-2012)
- Average household size: 2.46 persons (US Census Bureau, 2008-2012)

Data on the sector activity

- Number of water operators: NA
- Water main networks (km pipelines): NA
- Number of active connections (million): NA
- Abstracted water volume (million m³): NA
- Average consumption (litre/resident/day): 660 for the United States (Marques, 2010)
- Non-Revenue Water (in %): NA
- Turnover of the water industry (EUR): NA

Key facts of the water regulator

- Year of establishment: 1911
- Multi-sector regulator: Electricity, gas, motor carrier, railroad, telephone, water, wastewater
- Share of water operators covered: 16 operators (PUCO website)
- Budget: USD 71 646 302 (total) (EUR 51 million)
- Number of employees: 2 (water department)

For more information:
Public Utilities Commission of Ohio
180 East Broad Street
Columbus,
Ohio 43215
www.puco.ohio.gov/puco

Source: OECD Survey, 2014.

Institutional arrangements for water regulation

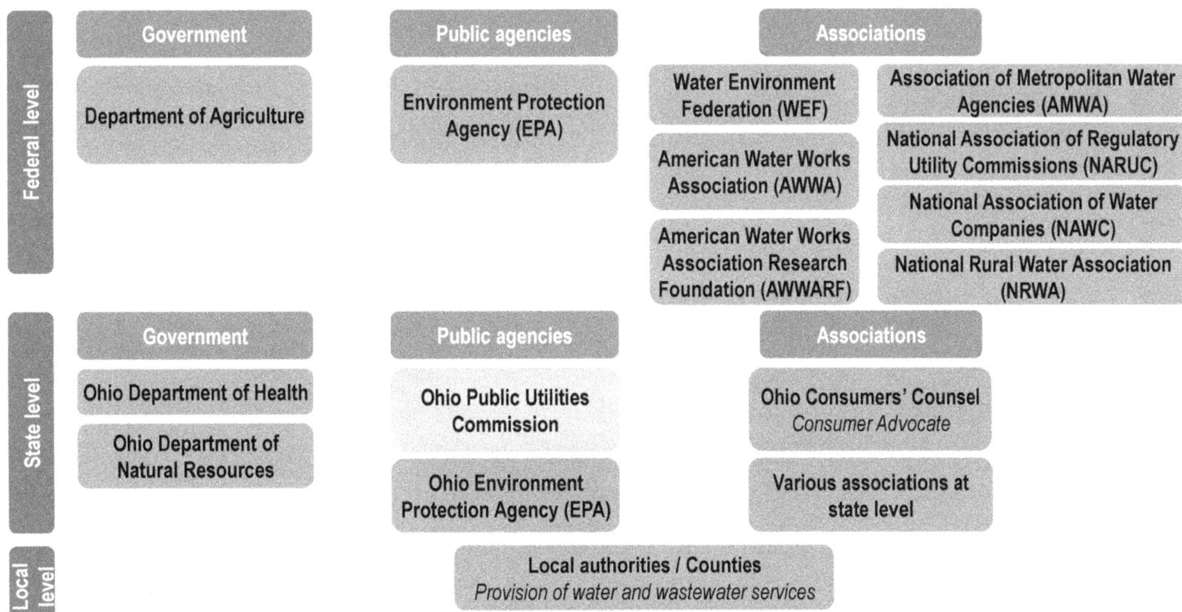

Sources: OECD Survey on the Governance of Water Regulators, 2014, Public Utilities Commission of Ohio: www.puco.ohio.gov/puco; US Census Bureau: http://quickfacts.census.gov/qfd/states/39000.html, "Elaborations on the metropolitan database"; OECD (2012), *Redefining "Urban": A New Way to Measure Metropolitan Areas*, OECD Publishing, Paris, http://dx.doi.org/10.1787/9789264174108-en; and Marques, R. (2010), *Regulation of Water and Wastewater Services – An International Comparison*, IWA Publishing, London.

UNITED STATES/PENNSYLVANIA

Key facts of the water sector

Territory

- Surface (km²): 119 283
- Population size (million): 12.773 (US Census Bureau, 2013 est.)
- Population density (inhabitants/km²): 110 (US Census Bureau, 2013 est.)
- Share of urban population: 58.5% of total population, 2010 (OECD, 2012)
- Number of households (million): 4.96 (US Census Bureau, 2008-2012)
- Average household size: 2.47 persons (US Census Bureau, 2008-2012)

Data on the sector activity

- Number of water operators: 2 100 (PUC website)
- Water main networks (km pipelines): NA
- Number of active connections (million): NA
- Abstracted water volume (million m³): NA
- Average consumption (litre/resident/day): 660 for the United States (Marques, 2010)
- Non-Revenue Water (in %): NA
- Turnover of the water industry (EUR): NA

Key facts of the water regulator

- Year of establishment: 1937
- Multi-sector regulator: Electricity, gas, water, wastewater, transportation
- Share of water operators covered: 6% (135 water and wastewater utilities, PUC website)
- Budget: USD 69 million (total) (EUR 50 million)
- Number of employees: approx. 10 (water regulation)

For more information:
Pennsylvania Public Utilities Commission
400 North Street
Keystone Bldg.
Harrisburg, PA 17120
www.puc.state.pa.us

Source: OECD Survey, 2014.

Institutional arrangements for water regulation

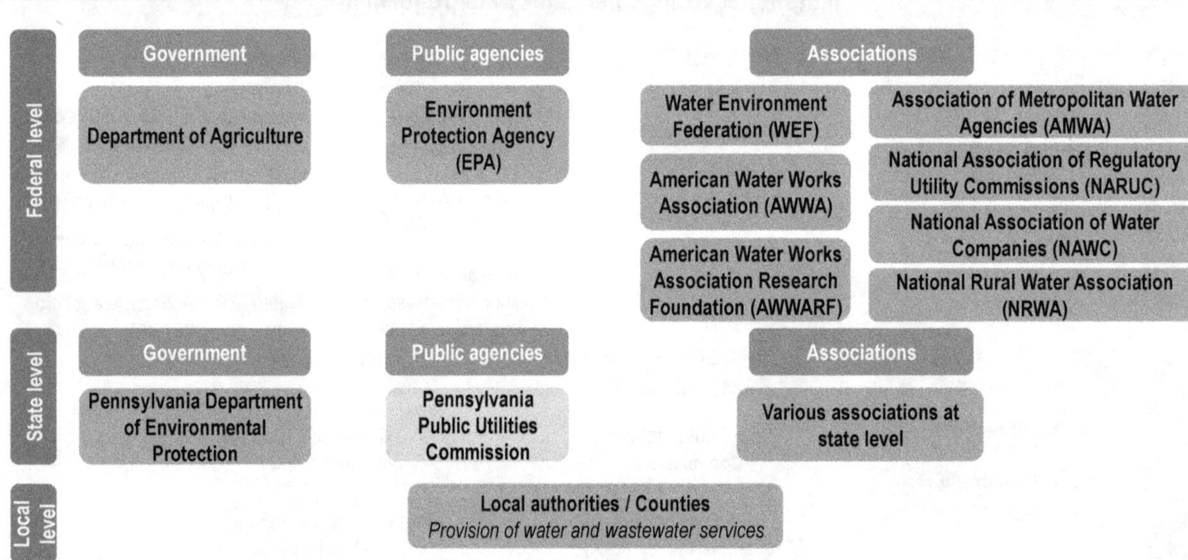

Sources: OECD Survey on the Governance of Water Regulators, 2014, Pennsylvania Public Utilities Commission: www.puc.state.pa.us; US Census Bureau: http://quickfacts.census.gov/qfd/states/42000.html, "Elaborations on the metropolitan database"; OECD (2012), *Redefining "Urban": A New Way to Measure Metropolitan Areas*, OECD Publishing, Paris, http://dx.doi.org/10.1787/9789264174108-en; and Marques, R. (2010), *Regulation of Water and Wastewater Services – An International Comparison*, IWA Publishing, London.

UNITED STATES/TENNESSEE

Key facts of the water sector

Territory

- Surface (km²): 109 247
- Population size (million): 6.496 (US Census Bureau, 2013 est.)
- Population density (inhabitants/km²): 60
- Share of urban population: 51.1% of total population, 2010 (OECD, 2012)
- Number of households (million): 2.469 (US Census Bureau, 2008-2012)
- Average household size: 2.51 persons (US Census Bureau, 2008-2012)

Data on the sector activity

- Number of water operators: >400 (OECD Survey, 2014)
- Water main networks (km pipelines): NA
- Number of active connections (million): NA
- Abstracted water volume (million m³): NA
- Average consumption (litre/resident/day): 660 for the United States (Marques, 2010)
- Non-Revenue Water (in %): NA
- Turnover of the water industry: (EUR 250 million – OECD Survey, 2014)

Key facts of the water regulator

- Year of establishment: 1995
- Multi-sector regulator: Telecom, water, wastewater, electricity, natural gas
- Share of water operators covered: 4% (19 water and wastewater utilities) (TRA Annual Report 2013/2014)
- Budget: USD 4.3 million (total) (EUR 6 million)
- Number of employees: 5 (water regulation)

For more information:
Tennessee Regulatory Authority
502 Deaderick Street | 4th Floor |
Nashville, TN 37243
www.state.tn.us/tra
Contact: contact.tra@tn.gov

Source: OECD Survey, 2014.

Institutional arrangements for water regulation

Federal level
- Government: Department of Agriculture
- Public agencies: Environment Protection Agency (EPA)
- Associations: Water Environment Federation (WEF); American Water Works Association (AWWA); American Water Works Association Research Foundation (AWWARF); Association of Metropolitan Water Agencies (AMWA); National Association of Regulatory Utility Commissions (NARUC); National Association of Water Companies (NAWC); National Rural Water Association (NRWA)

State level
- Government: Tennessee Department of Environment
- Public agencies: Tennessee Regulatory Authority
- Associations: Various associations at state level

Local level
- Local authorities /Counties
  Provision of water and wastewater services

Sources: OECD Survey on the Governance of Water Regulators, 2014, Tennessee Regulatory Authority: www.state.tn.us/tra; US Census Bureau: http://quickfacts.census.gov/qfd/states/47000.html; Elaborations on the metropolitan database; OECD (2012), *Redefining "Urban": A New Way to Measure Metropolitan Areas*, OECD Publishing, Paris, http://dx.doi.org/10.1787/9789264174108-en; and TRA Annual Report: www.state.tn.us/tra/reports/annualrpts/anlrpt1314.pdf; and Marques, R. (2010), *Regulation of Water and Wastewater Services – An International Comparison*, IWA Publishing, London.

UNITED STATES/WEST VIRGINIA

Key facts of the water sector

Territory

- Surface (km²): 62 755
- Population size (million): 1.854 (US Census Bureau, 2013 est.)
- Population density (inhabitants/km²): 29.8 (US Census Bureau, 2013 est.)
- Share of urban population: 9% of total population, 2010 (OECD, 2012)
- Number of households (million): 0.743 (US Census Bureau, 2008-2012)
- Average household size: 2.43 persons (US Census Bureau, 2008-2012)

Data on the sector activity

- Number of water operators: 550 (OECD Survey, 2014)
- Water main networks (km pipelines): NA
- Number of active connections (million): 0.6446
- Abstracted water volume (million m³): NA
- Average consumption (litre/resident/day): 660 for the United States (Marques, 2010)
- Non-Revenue Water (in %): NA
- Turnover of the water industry (EUR): 351.5 million (Marques, 2010)

Key facts of the water regulator

- Year of establishment: 1913
- Multi-sector regulator: Telecom, water, wastewater, electricity, natural gas
- Share of water operators covered: 100%
- Budget: USD 23 million (EUR18.2 million) (total)
- Number of employees: over 250 overall (approx. 30 in water regulation)

For more information:
Public Service Commission of West Virginia
201 Brooks Street
Charleston, WV 25301
www.psc.state.wv.us

Source: OECD Survey, 2014.

Institutional arrangements for water regulation

Federal level

- Government: Department of Agriculture
- Public agencies: Environment Protection Agency (EPA)
- Associations: Water Environment Federation (WEF); American Water Works Association (AWWA); American Water Works Association Research Foundation (AWWARF); Association of Metropolitan Water Agencies (AMWA); National Association of Regulatory Utility Commissions (NARUC); National Association of Water Companies (NAWC); National Rural Water Association (NRWA)

State level

- Government: West Virginia Department of Environmental Protection; West Virginia Bureau for Public Health
- Public agencies: West Virginia Public Service Commission (PSC)
- Associations: Various associations at state level

Local level

- Local authorities / Counties — *Provision of water and wastewater services*

Sources: OECD Survey on the Governance of Water Regulators, 2014, Public Service Commission of West Virginia: www.psc.state.wv.us; US Census Bureau: http://quickfacts.census.gov/qfd/states/54000.html. "Elaborations on the metropolitan database", OECD (2012), *Redefining "Urban": A New Way to Measure Metropolitan Areas*, OECD Publishing, Paris, http://dx.doi.org/10.1787/9789264174108-en; and Marques, R. (2010), *Regulation of Water and Wastewater Services – An International Comparison*, IWA Publishing, London.

URUGUAY

Key facts of the water sector

Territory

- Surface (km²): 176 215
- Population size (million): 3.402 (WB, 2013)
- Population density (inhabitants/km²): 19 (WB, 2013)
- Share of urban population: 91% of total population (ICPD, 2012)
- Number of households (million): 1.072 (UN Habitat, est. 2010)
- Average household size: 3.22 persons (UN Habitat, est. 2010)

Data on the sector activity

- Number of water operators: 3 (OECD Survey, 2014)
- Water main networks (km pipelines): 16 300
- Number of active connections (million): 1
- Abstracted water volume (million m³): 320 (Marques, 2010)
- Average consumption (litre/resident/day): 125 (Marques, 2010)
- Non-Revenue Water(in %): 48 (IBNET, 2011)
- Turnover of the water industry: UYU 10 billion (EUR 318 million – OECD Survey, 2014)

Key facts of the water regulator

- Year of establishment: 2002
- Multi-sector regulator: Energy – including oil and gas – and water
- Share of water operators covered: 100%
- Budget: UYU 80 million (total) (EUR 2.5 million)
  UYU 16 million (EUR 0.5 million) (water regulation)
- Number of employees: 4 (water regulation – the economic and legal staff is shared with energy)

For more information:
Unidad Reguladora Servicios Energia y Agua (URSEA)
1324 Piso 2, Torre Ejecutiva – Montevideo
www.ursea.gub.uy/inicio
Contact: consultas@ursea.gub.uy

Source: OECD Survey, 2014.

Institutional arrangements for water regulation

National level

Government	Public agencies	Water operator
Ministry of Economy and Finance *In charge of some aspects for tariff setting policy*	**Unidad Reguladora Servicios Energia y Agua (URSEA)**	**OSE (State Sanitary Works)** *Public operator in charge of water and sewage services (all country but Montevideo City for sewerage services)*
Ministry of Housing and Environment *Defines water policies*		
Office of Budget and Planning (OPP) *In charge of some aspects of investment definition*		

Local level

- **Intendencia de Montevideo (Montevideo City Government)** *Operates sewage services in Montevideo*
- **Municipalities**

Sources: OECD Survey on the Governance of Water Regulators, 2014, URSEA: www.ursea.gub.uy/inicio; IBNET: www.ib-net.org; ICPD: http://icpdbeyond2014.org/documents/download.php?f=final_uruguay.pdf; World Bank: www.data.worldbank.org/country/uruguay; UN Habitat: http://ww2.unhabitat.org/habrdd/conditions/southamerica/uruguay.htm.

Annex A

Participants in the OECD Survey on the Governance of Water Regulators

	Territory	Name of the regulator
1	Albania	Water Regulatory Authority of Albania
2	Armenia	Public Services Regulatory Commission of the Republic of Armenia (PSRC)
3	Australia/Capital Territory (ACT)	Independent Competition and Regulatory Commission (ICRC)
4	Australia/New South Wales (NSW)	Independent Pricing and Regulatory Tribunal (IPART)
5	Australia/Victoria	Essential Services Commission
6	Australia/Western Australia (WA)	Economic Regulation Authority (ERAWA)
7	Belgium/Flanders	Water Regulator – Flemish Environment Agency
8	Brazil/Rio Grande do Sul (RS)	Agência Estadual de Regulação dos Serviços Públicos, Delegados do Rio Grande do Sul (AGERGS)
9	Bulgaria	State Energy and Water Regulatory Commission (SEWRC)
10	Chile	Superintendencia de Servicio Sanitarios (SISS)
11	Colombia	Regulatory Commission for Water and Sanitation (CRA)
12	Estonia	Competition Authority
13	Hungary	Hungarian Energy and Public Utility Regulatory Authority
14	Indonesia	Jakarta Water Supply Regulatory Body
15	Ireland	Commission for Energy Regulation (CER)
16	Italy	Regulatory Authority for Electricity, Gas and Water (AEEGSI)
17	Kosovo	Water and Wastewater Regulatory Office of Kosovo (WWRO)
18	Latvia	Public Utilities Commission of Latvia (PUC)
19	Malaysia	National Water Services Commission
20	Mozambique	Water and Sanitation Regulatory Council (CRA)
21	Peru	Superintendencia Nacional de Servicios de Saneamiento (SUNASS)
22	Portugal	The Water and Waste Services Regulation Authority (ERSAR)
23	Romania	National Regulatory Authority for Municipal Services (ANRSC)
24	UK/England & Wales	Water Services Regulation Authority (OFWAT)
25	UK/Northern Ireland	Northern Ireland Authority for Utility Regulator (NIAUR)
26	UK/Scotland	Water Industry Commission for Scotland (WISC)
27	Ukraine	National Commission of the State Public Utilities Regulation of Ukraine (SCWRM)
28	USA/Hawaii	Hawaii Public Utilities Commission
29	USA/Maine	Maine Public Utilities Commission
30	USA/Ohio	Public Utilities Commission of Ohio
31	USA/Pennsylvania	Pennsylvanian Public Utility Commission
32	USA/Tennessee	Tennessee Regulatory Authority
33	USA/West Virginia	Public Service Commission of West Virginia
34	Uruguay	Unidad Reguladora Servicios Energia y Agua (URSEA)

Annex B

Water tariff setting methodologies in selected territories

Summary table: retail tariff methodology

	Frequency of tariff setting (years)	Cost plus	Price cap	Consideration of revenue (number & affordability of customers)	Profit regulation	Consideration of Performance	Other
Albania		+				+	
Australia/Capital Territory	6	+		+		+	
Australia/NSW	4		+	+			
Australia/Victoria	5	+		+			
Bulgaria			+				
Chile	5	+					+
Estonia	°	+					
Hungary	1	+				+	
Ireland	6		+			*	
Italy	4				+		+
Kosovo	3	+					
Latvia		+			+		
Mozambique		+				+	
Peru	5	+		+		+	
Portugal	1	+			+	+	
Romania	°	+					
UK/England and Wales	5		+				
UK/Northern Ireland	6		+				
UK/Scotland	6		+				
Ukraine		+					
US/Hawaii		+					
US/Ohio		+					
US/Pennsylvania		+					
US/Tennessee		+					
Uruguay	1	+					

° At the request of the water companies.

+ In use.

* Under consideration.

In **Albania**, tariff regulation takes into consideration the progress made by water utilities towards improved technical and financial performance. Tariff setting follows the steps below:

- Proposal by water utilities supported by opinion of local government units
- Cost analysis (deduction of unacceptable cost)
- Performance analysis (performance adjustments)
- Setting of tariff level (average tariff)
- Setting of tariff structure (tariff categories)

In **Australia/ICRC**, the methodology is set by the Commission and may be different for each regulatory period. Currently the regulatory period is 6 years with a CPI adjustment for the even years (2, 4 and 6) and a more thorough biennial recalibration (consideration of capex/opex and other factors) of the price for the even years (3 and 5).

In **Australia**, both IPART in New South Wales and the Essential Services Commission in Victoria use a "building block" methodology. It involves estimating a water authority's required revenue for a regulatory period. This estimate includes an assessment of efficient capital and operating costs that reflect delivery of a water authority's service obligations. Maximum prices are then set based on this building block revenue and numbers of customers.

In **Bulgaria**, for the period 2009-2013 a "Price cap" approach is used where SEWRC approves prices for water and sewerage operator for the first year of the regulatory period and changes them at the end of each year to account for inflation, but also decrease by a factor to improve the efficiency of water and sewerage operator.

In **Chile**, tariffs are calculated on the basis of an efficient model company and considering a long-term total cost (investment, replacement, maintenance, operation, management) with a rate of return calculated by a methodology fixed by law.

In **Hungary**, the price is determined for each water utility supplier or water utility system, using a comparative economic analysis on costs, prices and fees, also considering the following aspects:

- the prices shall encourage safe water utility supply at the lowest cost, the improvement of the efficiency of management, the effective use of capacities, the continuous improvement of the quality of supply and the observation of the principle of preserving natural resources;
- the allowable costs of continuous and safe water utility supply shall be taken into account, as well as the allowable costs of performing environmental obligations, especially including the allowable costs of water base protection.

In **Italy**, the methodology is based on the full cost recovery principle and efficient reference values, in addition to polluter pays principle and the need to incentivise water saving. This principle is declined through a matrix of Regulatory Schemes, combining parametric and standard evaluations, revenue cap methodology and limited cases of tariff boost where urgent extra-investments are required.

In **Kosovo**, the methodology used evaluates the cash request that service providers need to cover annual expenses and a rate of return on capital. Tariffs are determined for a period of three years. They are revised every year to account for inflation and the achievement of objectives set for the previous year. Service providers are entitled to request a review of existing tariffs, when the business circumstances are influenced by internal or external factors.

In **Latvia**, tariff setting is based on full cost recovery plus a profit margin which cannot exceed 7% of the total expenses. The tariff shall include the depreciation of the fixed assets; the operational costs including staff, repair and other costs of economic activities (materials, electricity), costs related to the control of the state of the environment, expenditure related to guarding, transport maintenance, insurance, communications and other expenses.

In **Peru**, tariffs are calculated using a long-term planning tool (30 years) called the Optimized Master Plan. This tool simultaneously sets management goals for increasing coverage, quality improvement and programming efficiency investments, as well as the operating and maintenance costs to achieve these goals. The tariffs and the associated management goals are set for a 5-year period.

In **Portugal**, there are two different methodologies for tariff setting: one for bulk operators and one for retail operators. Currently, bulk tariffs are defined by the regulator following a "cost plus" methodology based on an analysis of the provisional costs which are analyzed considering efficient service provision. In the future, it is expected that this methodology will change for a "revenue cap" model, in order to provide incentives for efficiency to the operators. For the state-owned bulk operators, the investments are evaluated by ERSAR in the beginning of each new regulatory period. In relation to retail services, it is expected that ERSAR will soon issue a binding regulation that establishes the principles of tariff setting that the municipalities and retail operators must follow in defining the tariff values and structures. If they do not follow this regulation, ERSAR has the power to enforce the compliance with this regulation.

In **UK/England and Wales**, OFWAT reviews company plans on a five-year cycle, using incentive-based regulation to encourage efficiencies and drive down costs. Companies provide a statement each year setting out their tariffs for the year ahead. OFWAT has finalised a new approach to setting price controls that will be applied for the period 2015-20: www.ofwat.gov.uk/pricereview/pr14/prs_web201307finalapproach.

In **UK/Scotland**, WICS assesses the investment plan every six years with a rolling review every three years. Prices are set using incentive-based regulation and targeting a suite of financial indicators. *Financial tramlines* provide a mechanism to share any outperformance with customers, monitor financial strength and reduce risk. Household customers are unmetered in Scotland so tariffs are fixed and based on the council tax banding system and its discounts to ensure that charges are set in a progressive and affordable manner.

In **Ukraine**, tariff setting follows a "cost plus" methodology. Utilities submit their tariff calculations based on cost data for costs incurred in the reporting year and the anticipated costs for the coming year. They also submit investment plans and the proposed sources for funding those investments. The investments are funded mostly by the cumulated depreciation, loan financing and profit component. Profit is determined as the amount of money that exceeds the full planned cost.

Source: OECD (2014), Survey on Applying Better Regulation in the Water Service Sector.

Annex C

Selected examples of water performance indicators

In Bulgaria, the regulator collects performance information on the following 15 indicators which are listed in the *Law on Regulation of the Water Supply and Sewerage Services* (Chapter 3, Article 9):

1. Penetration of water-supply services;
2. Drinking water quality;
3. Non-interruption of water supply (uninterrupted water delivery and duration of disruptions);
4. Total water losses in the water-supply systems and time limits for the reduction thereof;
5. Breakdowns of the water-supply system;
6. Pressure in the water-supply system;
7. Penetration of sewerage services;
8. Quality of raw waste water and of treated waste water;
9. Breakdowns of the sewerage system;
10. Floods in properties of third persons caused by the sewerage;
11. Operational indicators of efficiency;
12. Financial indicators of efficiency;
13. Time limit for reaction to written complaints by consumers;
14. Time limit for connecting new consumers with the water-supply and sewer systems;
15. Staff size in proportion to the number of consumers serviced.

These 15 key indicators are further elaborated into 49 sub indicators (cf. Annex No. 1 of the Ordinance of long-term rates, terms and conditions for the formation of the annual target levels of quality water and wastewater services) which are themselves further developed into 72 performance indicators (cf. Guidelines to the implementation of the above Ordinance, Annex 2). The key indicators and their sub-indicators are part of the business plans of WWS operators in Bulgaria.

In UK/England and Wales, the indicators are grouped into four high-level areas, for which OFWAT has set out *i)* a brief definition of the indicator; *ii)* relevant obligations that relate to the indicator; *iii)* how the indicator should be calculated; *iv)* the minimum frequency of reporting; *iv)* any targets set for the indicator; and where relevant, appropriate tolerances for the indicator.

1. Customer experience:	• Service incentive mechanism (SIM) • Internal sewer flooding • Water supply interruptions
2. Reliability and availability:	• Serviceability water non-infrastructure • Serviceability water infrastructure • Serviceability sewerage non-infrastructure • Serviceability sewerage infrastructure • Leakage • Security of supply index
3. Environmental impact:	• Greenhouse gas emissions • Pollution incidents (sewerage) • Serious pollution incidents (sewerage) • Pollution incidents (water) • Discharge permit compliance • Satisfactory sludge disposal
4. Financial:	• Post-tax return on capital • Credit rating • Gearing • Interest cover

Sources: OECD Survey on Applying Better Regulation in the Water Service Sector (2014) and OECD (2013).

In Peru, 35 performance indicators are grouped into two high-level areas: Provision of services and Business Management. Every high-level has three sub-levels and two sub-levels, respectively. These are:

1. Provision of services:	• Quality of service delivery	– Presence of residual chlorine – Presence of thermotolerant coliform – Turbidity – Continuity – Pressure – Total density claims – Wastewater Treatment
	• Billing	– Average rate – Average billing – Unit consumption measured – Unit volume billed
	• Affordability	– Potable water coverage – Sewerage coverage

2. Business management:	• Sustainability of services	– Working relationship – Replacement of fixed assets – Maintenance costs of infrastructure – Current liquidity – Indebtedness – Interest coverage – Operating margin – Return on assets (ROA) – Return on equity (ROE)
	• Business efficiency	– Non- revenue water – Micrometering – Active connections billed by metering – Default ratio – Operating cost per unit volume produced – Operating cost per unit volume billed – Produced water obtained from underground sources – Produced volume per unit – Staff costs per unit volume billed – Sales and service costs per unit volume billed – Density of breaks in the distribution networks potable water – Density of sewer blockages

Some of these performance indicators are used to set the management goals of the water companies. The main management goals are related to increasing coverage and improvement of the service quality such as:

- Household potable water connections
- Household sewer connections
- Annual increase in new water meters
- Water unbilled
- Pressure
- Continuity
- Wastewater treatment
- Update of technical and commercial cadastre
- Density of breaks in the distribution networks potable water

- Density of sewer blockages

The tariff increases authorised by the Regulator are subject to compliance of these management goals.

In Portugal, the indicators are grouped into three high-level areas: Protection of user interests, Operator sustainability, and Environmental sustainability. ERSAR has created a Technical guide which establishes all the definitions for the data and the indicators, and the methodologies to collect the information. For each of the 16 indicators per service there are reference brackets that define if the service is good, average or unsatisfactory. The process, from the collection, in office validation and on site auditing of all the information provided, until the disclosure of the information to the general public, follows an annual cycle.

Drinking Water Services indicators

1. Protection of user interests	• Accessibility of service for users – Physical accessibility of the service – Affordability of the service • Quality of service provided to users – Service interruptions – Safe water – Reply to written suggestions and complaints
2. Operator sustainability	• Economic sustainability – Cost recovery ratio – Connection to the service – Non-revenue water • Infrastructural sustainability – Adequacy of treatment capacity – Mains rehabilitation – Mains failures • Physical productivity of human resources – Adequacy of human resources
3. Environmental sustainability	• Efficient use of environmental resources – Real water losses – Fulfilment of the water abstraction licensing – Standardised energy consumption • Efficiency in pollution prevention – Sludge disposal

Wastewater Services indicators

1. Protection of user interests	• Accessibility of service for users – Physical accessibility of the service – Affordability of the service • Quality of service provided to users

	– Flooding occurrences – Reply to written suggestions and complaints
2. Operator sustainability	• Economic sustainability – Cost recovery ratio – Connection to the service • Infrastructural sustainability – Adequacy of treatment capacity – Sewer rehabilitation – Sewer collapses • Physical productivity of human resources – Adequacy of human resources
3. Environmental sustainability	• Efficient use of environmental resources – Standardised energy consumption • Efficiency in pollution prevention – Proper treatment of collected wastewater – Emergency control discharges – Wastewater analysis – Compliance of discharge parameters – Sludge disposal

Glossary

Administrative burdens: The costs imposed on water operators/water consumers when complying with information obligations stemming from regulation of water and wastewater services. They include the costs involved in obtaining, reading and understanding regulations, developing compliance strategies and meeting mandated reporting requirements, including data collection, processing, reporting on storage, but do not include the capital costs measures taken to comply with the regulations, not the costs to the public sector of administering regulations.

Commission model: the board itself makes most substantive regulatory decisions – examples include the United State's Federal Trade Commission and the Australian Competition and Consumer Commission.

Governance board model: the board is primarily responsible for the oversight, strategic guidance and operational policy of the regulator, with regulatory decision-making functions largely delegated the chief executive officer (CEO) and staff – for example, the United Kingdom's OFWAT (Water Services Regulation Authority).

Independent regulator: A regulator whose role and powers have been established in legislation and who makes regulatory decisions at arm's length from executive government. An independent regulator is not subject to the direction on individual regulatory decisions by executive government, but could be supported by officials who are located within a Ministry.

Regulation: The term regulation covers the diverse set of instruments by which governments impose requirements on enterprises and citizens. Regulations include all primary laws, formal and informal orders, subordinate regulations, administrative formalities and rules issued by non-governmental or self-regulatory bodies to whom governments have delegated regulatory powers.

Regulators / regulatory agencies: Administrators in government departments and other agencies responsible for making regulations.

Regulatory Impact Analysis (RIA): Systematic process of identification and quantification of important benefits and costs likely to flow from the adoption of a proposed regulation or a non-regulatory policy option under consideration. May be based on benefit/ cost analysis, cost effectiveness analysis, business impact analysis etc.

Single member regulator: An individual is appointed as regulator and makes most substantive regulatory decisions and delegates other decisions to its staff.

Statement of expectation: A document provided by the minister to the regulator. Each statement outlines relevant government policies, including the government's current objectives relevant to the regulator, and any expectations on how the regulator should conduct its operations.

ORGANISATION FOR ECONOMIC CO-OPERATION AND DEVELOPMENT

The OECD is a unique forum where governments work together to address the economic, social and environmental challenges of globalisation. The OECD is also at the forefront of efforts to understand and to help governments respond to new developments and concerns, such as corporate governance, the information economy and the challenges of an ageing population. The Organisation provides a setting where governments can compare policy experiences, seek answers to common problems, identify good practice and work to co-ordinate domestic and international policies.

The OECD member countries are: Australia, Austria, Belgium, Canada, Chile, the Czech Republic, Denmark, Estonia, Finland, France, Germany, Greece, Hungary, Iceland, Ireland, Israel, Italy, Japan, Korea, Luxembourg, Mexico, the Netherlands, New Zealand, Norway, Poland, Portugal, the Slovak Republic, Slovenia, Spain, Sweden, Switzerland, Turkey, the United Kingdom and the United States. The European Commission takes part in the work of the OECD.

OECD Publishing disseminates widely the results of the Organisation's statistics gathering and research on economic, social and environmental issues, as well as the conventions, guidelines and standards agreed by its members.

OECD PUBLISHING, 2, rue André-Pascal, 75775 PARIS CEDEX 16
(42 2015 04 1 P) ISBN 978-92-64-23108-5 – 2015-07

www.ingramcontent.com/pod-product-compliance
Lightning Source LLC
LaVergne TN
LVHW081411110826
845149LV00010B/1701

* 9 7 8 9 2 6 4 2 3 1 0 8 5 *